SAI

Michael Marshall is a for
Director of the Anglican
was appointed by the A
with Michael Green in la
for the Decade of Evangelism in autumn 1992. Among
numerous popular books on spirituality and theology, he
has written *Change of Heart* (1988), *Just Like Him!* (1988) and
Great Expectations? (1991). He is a columnist for the *Church of
England Newspaper*.

John Feaan

Confirmed 18 - 5 - 1993
by + Peter Malmesbury
God himself confirmed
the apostles' witness......
by distributing the
Gifts of the Holy Spirit
in the various ways
he wills

Hebrews, 2⁴

Dedicated to
all the Anonymous Saints
who are known to God alone;
whose lives have enriched
our world, and whose continuing
prayers in heaven renew,
support and protect God's
church on earth.

SAINTS ALIVE!

Biblical Reflections
on the Lives of the Saints

Michael Marshall

TRi/\NGlE

First published in Great Britain 1992
Triangle
SPCK
Holy Trinity Church
Marylebone Road
London NW1 4DU

First published in the USA 1992
by Morehouse Publishing

British Library Cataloguing in Publication Data
A catalogue record for this book is available
from the British Library

ISBN 0-281-04572-0

Printed in Great Britain by
BPCC Hazells Ltd
Member of BPCC Ltd

Contents

Acknowledgments

I am deeply honored to have some small part in the very special celebrations in the Anglican diocese of Europe as they celebrate, in 1992, one hundred and fifty years of Anglican witness and life on that continent. The unity and re-formation of Europe will undoubtedly be one of the most striking political features of the beginning of the twenty-first century. The sudden collapse of Communism in Eastern Europe in the last decade of the twentieth century should encourage Christians of all persuasions to work together for spiritual renewal and for a genuine "perestroika" in every aspect of European life. We should pray and work to see that Anglican Christians make a generous and strategic contribution to the spiritual reawakening of the continent of Europe.

I would wish to thank Bishop John Satterthwaite for inviting me to write this Lent book, which will be studied by the parishes in the various parts of his large and diverse diocese. The Rev. John Rowlands has worked patiently with me from the outset of this whole enterprise, and I am most grateful to him for his encouragement and support at all times.

Mr. Allen Kelley of Morehouse Publishing has gone that second mile in making the necessarily speedy production of this book possible and in being so accommodating to the author as he struggled with the manuscript! Jan Boudinet was the essential wordsmith, and in many ways is the untitled author of this book. She introduced the titled author to the art of the computer keyboard during the production of this book! Certainly, without her patient and hardworking oversight, the book simply could not have been produced.

I am truly grateful to her, as also to Ann Muehlmann, who worked especially hard on the manuscript. Sally Barrett gave most valuable advice and help in editing this book, as she has done with so many of my previous writings.

Introducing the Saints

"The world needs saints, just as a plague-stricken city needs doctors." (Simone Weil)

"What is a saint?" somebody once asked. "A saint is someone who lived a long time ago, who has never been adequately researched!" Presumably, the implication behind that reply was that, if you researched a saint long enough, sooner or later you would find that he or she had—as we like to say—"feet of clay."

We sometimes speak somewhat dangerously of the saints as being "the heroes of faith." Yet, the communion of saints has nothing whatever to do with the cult of hero worship. We put heroes on pedestals or plinths, and then, after subsequent "adequate" research, we find that their human frailties and weaknesses are much the same as those of lesser mortals like ourselves. We become cynical and we feel let down. "We have seen through them," we say. It is not long before we tear our heroes off their pedestals and bury them beneath the rubble of our disappointment, disillusionment, and even cynicism.

Saints are the very opposite of heroes. You are supposed to be able to see right through the saints. They are intended to be gloriously transparent, which is why the church delights to put them in stained glass windows! We do that precisely because we are intended to see through them, and what we see through them is the light that shines through them from beyond.

For in the Western church, it is required that a saint has been so hollowed out—generally through suffering—that God can work at least three miracles right through them! Such is the difference, then, between heroes and saints. It parallels the difference between virtue and holiness.

You can be born virtuous or you can acquire it, or even (like Shakespeare's "greatness") have it "thrust upon" you. You cannot acquire holiness. Holiness, like that other elusive reality—grace—is the raw material from which saints are made, but it is supremely, from start to finish, a gift. You can receive it, but you can never achieve it. Furthermore, you may well have met a saint and never recognized him or her for what they truly were. For Paul is right when he reminds us that we have this "treasure in earthen vessels." Saints are not what they seem to be. They are not very good at keeping up appearances, and they are certainly not in the business of trying to *impress* anybody, quite simply because they are too busy trying to *express* to everybody something of that love which possesses them and which flows right through them.

So, "What is a saint?" was probably, after all, the wrong way to frame the question. "Who are the saints?" might be a better way to put the question. We tend to think of them corporately (though certainly not collectively). Furthermore, part of their fascination is that they are most certainly very personal and, in some sense, they are personalities without ever trying to pursue the cult of individualism. Therefore, the church delights to speak of the "communion of saints." For one thing is absolutely certain. The saints are never cloned: they are all as different and unique as fingerprints. In fact, it is very difficult to discover whether this "communion" has anything at all in common! Among the twelve apostles, there is a diversity which, upon the surface, appears to be potentially and dangerously explosive. How on earth (literally) is Matthew, who worked for the occupying forces of the Romans, supposed to get along with the zealous and patriotic apostles like James and John? What does Peter, a fisherman from the north, have in common with that university professor, Paul, who has studied and traveled extensively? But it does not stop there. When you read the lives of the saints in the small collection in this volume, you will realize that there is no particular kind of personality which is more susceptible to sanctity than any other. Myers-Briggs would have real problems in classifying the personalities of the saints; for grace can and does work on any kind of raw material and convert it to sanctity. Furthermore, what is essentially distinctive in that natural raw material (inherited in genes or conditioned by environment) is not lost in conversion, reduced, or even flattened out in the process of sanctity. Camillus de Lellis, Catherine of Siena, Margaret of Cortona, and Gregory the Great represent many different varieties of personality makeup and come from many different backgrounds. Yet, all show a facet of the great Divine Love; all have a slightly different emphasis, and all draw out for us the many-sided, multidimensional nature of love.

Their unity in their diversity is obvious in only one respect. They all point away from themselves and are all caught up in something beyond themselves. They are all looking to the one Christ, and in him they have all found their needs supplied and their yearnings fulfilled.

So we are not asked either to worship the saints as though they were heroes, or to try to copy them. Yet we are asked to *celebrate* the saints. God is glorified in and through his saints. It is the need to celebrate the saints which has created the calendar of the Christian year. It's as though there is—as, indeed, there truly is—too much here to take in at one go. A little like a large picture gallery, full of the works of the masters, a review of the saints demands that we walk slowly through the gallery, stopping and pausing to catch more of the color, the light, and the shadow. The Christian disciple will take time to study, reflect upon, but, above all, to celebrate in the course of a year, the glory of the saints, which itself is a reflection of the glory of God.

Each age will be struck by the different characteristics of the one Christ, manifested in the faces of his many saints. In an age of liberation movements of various kinds, what has struck the author of this book most forcefully has been the wide margin of freedom which is evident on every page of the lives of the saints. The saints really do refuse to be conformed to this world or to any one culture. They refuse to be categorized or labelled. They refuse to talk endlessly about their problems in self-conscious discussions. They are not the prisoners of any particular ideology, either political, psychological, or social. Their lives are full of surprise. "The holiness of God is always what we least expected," comments A.M. Allchin. The saints have more than the average measure of absurdity in their lives. You cannot fence them in, and yet they refuse to be kept out or just drop out. They are walking contradictions of everything we have ever accepted as unquestionably true and proven. They are, in fact, the exceptions which prove the rule. They are clearly larger than life and, in a real sense, too big (rather than too good) for this world. They give the impression, not that they find the world too enticing, but rather that they find it far too boring and predictable by half. Naturally, they refuse to settle down, because at some point they have clearly been right down, and now they are being raised up too far ever to settle down again. Yet, in all of this there is nothing contrived, programmed, or predictable.

In a word, holiness is fascinating and saints are fabulous people. So, perhaps, Charles Péguy was right after all, when he said, "The only real disappointment in life is not to have been a saint."

Sadly, most of us will settle for the next best thing, though that is the kind of plausible advice which the saints themselves always refuse to take. We will just try to get to know the saints a little. This book is an attempt to whet the appetite of Christians who, in the words of the catholic creeds, claim to believe in the communion of saints, the forgiveness of sins, and the resurrection of the body. In a sense, those last clauses of the creeds are a package deal. I suspect that I could not believe in the possibility of sanctity if I had not experienced, and believed in, the infinite forgiveness of my sins. At the same time, bodily resurrection will simply make explicit and evident what has been problematical since the dawn of time, and will show to the whole creation that the way of resurrection via the cross is, indeed, the Way in which, in the end, all things can work together for good for those who believe in the grace and love of God.

My selection of saints is, of course, arbitrary, a little erratic, and quite indefensible. I have put in my list some that many would choose to ignore, and I am guilty, I fear, of ignoring the "big hitters." For example, I have included saints from the Anglican calendar, and we all know that in Anglicanism we do not officially "make" saints. It is my hope that some readers will be intrigued to discover names in this list that they have never seen before. Not maliciously, and for no obvious reason, I have not included any saints from America, while at the same time, I have also excluded both St. John of the Cross and St. Teresa of Avila—and again, all this is from no preconceived motive.

I hope that this collection of saints will capture the interest of readers so that they will be led to further research (though I suspect never "adequate research!") which, in its turn, will lead to a new intimacy with that great fellowship of those who have gone ahead of us in the way of faith, of grace, and of love. I hope that this book will be used to open the eyes of many to the riches of God's grace, to the potential and challenge of holiness, but above all, to a new commitment to a renewal in holiness and to living out the rich and full implications of our baptismal life.

For, at the liturgy of Easter Eve, the whole church is renewed around the font of baptism and the new Christians are baptized. As those who are to be baptized are taken to the font in procession, it is traditional for the church to sing the Litany of the Saints. It is a powerful moment and a glorious vision. The church on earth calls out to the far ends of eternity and invites the saints of God from every age to witness the new life of new Christians here on earth, and to support and encourage these new Christians in their earthly pilgrimage. For we are indeed surrounded with a great cloud of witnesses, who have a continuing interest in and passionate love for our world. (That was always their problem—they loved the world so much, but in the end they loved its Creator more than all.) Yet, they want so much to see the renewal of the church in our day. We need their prayers, their support and their continuing encouragement to help in God's glorious scheme and plan for the redemption of the whole world.

> Let saints on earth in concert sing
> With those whose work is done;
> For all the servants of our King
> In earth and heaven are one.
> (C. Wesley)

How to Use This Book

This book was originally commissioned as a Lenten Bible study book to be used either in daily Bible study or in Bible study groups during the six weeks of Lent leading up to Holy Week and Easter. It can, however, be used in any six-week period.

There is much talk today about the renewal of the church. There is also much evidence that God is, indeed, renewing his church in our day. This book is intended to be itself a kind of six-week program in renewal, based upon the vision of Isaiah and divided into six sections.

Each section has a passage of Scripture; a brief exposition of the biblical passage which is then matched by a very brief biography of a saint. Each section concludes with a reflection upon what we can learn from the previous ingredients at the level of human experience. Each week has an introduction to the theme of the week and concludes with some suggested questions which may help to ferment personal reflection or discussion in the groups.

Anglicanism discerns and distills its theology from Scripture, tradition, reason, and experience. The saints are the embodiment of tradition, and experience is intended to be that inner life of the spirit which should help to guide all Christians in the way of truth and in the way of Christ.

It is also intended that such a little book as this might be a simple resource book for spiritual direction and for those concerned with Christian formation. Isaiah's vision in the first eight verses of his sixth chapter is a classical model for personal and corporate renewal in faith and holiness. It bears our patient study, reflection, and meditation to draw out the essential ingredients of Christian discipleship.

In the year that King Uzziah died I saw the Lord sitting upon a throne, high and lifted up; and his train filled the temple. Above him stood the seraphim; each had six wings: with two he covered his face, and with two he covered his feet, and with two he flew. And one called to another and said: "Holy, holy, holy is the Lord of hosts; the whole earth is full of his glory." And the foundations of the thresholds shook at the voice of him who called, and the house was filled with smoke. And I said: "Woe is me! For I am lost; for I am a man of unclean lips, and I dwell in the midst of a people of unclean lips; for my eyes have seen the King, the Lord of hosts!" Then flew one of the seraphim to me, having in his hand a burning coal which he had taken with tongs from the altar. And he touched my mouth, and said: "Behold, this has touched your lips; your guilt is taken away, and your sin is forgiven." And I heard the voice of the Lord saying, "Whom shall I send, and who will go for us?" Then I said, "Here I am! Send me."

(Isa. 6:1–8)

The Gift of Vision

In the year that King Uzziah died I saw the Lord sitting upon a throne, high and lifted up; and his train filled the temple.

INTRODUCING WEEK ONE

"Where there is no vision, the people perish" (Prov. 29:18). The church is renewed by the continuing gift of Christ to his people, and true renewal, both personal and corporate begins when vision is granted and eyes are opened.

The year that King Uzziah died (about 740 BC) was the beginning of a new chapter for the people of Israel. In that year of the "bad news," the prophet was perceptive enough to be able to see the "good news." We often find the two opposites in the same place and at the same time. In place of the old king who had just died, the prophet Isaiah, in the temple, was granted a vision of *the* King, the real King, the eternal King—the Lord of hosts—and from that moment, renewal began. *Le roi est mort: vive le Roi!* The prophet is at pains to point out that the death of the old king coincided with his vision of the true King, the Lord of hosts. It so happens that the reign of King Uzziah had been one of security, stability, and prosperity. Isaiah, who was possibly a courtier, had probably become fixated with the old king, and this, if it were so, would have blinded him and God's people also to the eternal presence of the real King—the Lord of hosts—who eternally rules the universe and whose reign is without end. The character of the earthly king serves us best if, like an icon, he points beyond himself to the heavenly King. Uzziah's failure to do that had involved God's people in the worship of other gods and had blinded them to the claims of the eternal King.

In any event, Isaiah sees for the first time something which had been there all the time, staring him in the face. He was too blind to see it, because a false security had given him no incentive to look hard enough. The real King was holy and demanded Isaiah's total worship. (Perhaps some of this had been transferred to the shadow king, Uzziah, during those years of false security and vanity fair.) Isaiah, the courtier, could be forgiven for thinking that the bottom had fallen out of his world when the long and prestigious reign of Uzziah finished. In fact, it turned out not to be the end of anything of eternal significance. Rather, it was the beginning of everything of lasting significance for Isaiah, the courtier turned prophet.

So suddenly, as we say, "the penny dropped." At times of vision such as this, when we suddenly have a totally new insight into the real shape of things, we often exclaim, "Now I see," and frequently we preface the remark with the divine name: "My God, now I see!" It is not that we see a different world, but rather that we see the same old world very differently—in a new light, and a new perspective. Shakespeare, in his play *King Lear*, refers to God's people as "God's spies"—and so, in a sense, they are, if they are true to their contemplative and prayerful calling. The spectator sees most of the game, and so it is with the contemplatives who really see the world for what it is and for what it could become. It is the contemplatives—men and women of vision—who really make a difference in the world. They have a vision. So all Christians are called to go frequently into the "temple" or some holy place to look, to listen, and to wait upon the Lord. Isaiah tells us from his own experience that "those that wait upon the Lord shall renew their strength" (Isa. 40:31).

In the early church, the new Christians who were being prepared for baptism during Lent and leading up to Easter would be anointed by the bishop. He would touch their eyelids and put his fingers into their ears, repeating the word of Jesus, "*Ephphatha*—be open." In this way, he would anoint with holy oil their senses so that they may, by God's grace, be made more aware and become more sensitive to the word of God, to the vision of God, and to the touch of God.

So, whether we are seeking renewal personally or for a parish congregation (and we should be doing both of these all the time), we need to realize the prime importance of vision—that new insight which alone can bring a totally new outlook upon the whole of life, leading, as it does, to repentance and renewal.

Yet, all of this is the Lord's doing. Our part is to keep our eyes open and our ears ready to hear. Spiritual shortsightedness will lead us to turn inward in a wrongly introspective way, turning molehills into mountains; being blind to the wood for the trees; unable to see the larger picture, perpetually confusing means and ends and tactics with strategy. On the other hand, spiritual longsightedness tempts us to escape into generalities, programs, schemes, and projects, while we remain blind to the familiar figure of Lazarus sitting right there on our very doorstep!

So it will take vision to bring focus to mission, witness, and service. We need to be kept on our toes, as we stretch to look over the top of distractions and obstructions to that glory which is always there, whether we see it or not, and which is always just beyond our reach, over the next horizon where God is preparing our true future.

Questions for Personal Reflection or Discussion in Groups

1. What place do retreats have in my spiritual journey and in the life of the parish?
2. What are some of the positive lessons to be learned in times of bereavement, and in what ways do close attachments to people or things blind us to a proper commitment to God "in and above all things?"
3. Is there enough space and time in my life for reflection on looking for, and waiting upon God for his gifts and his graces?
4. Do I keep a spiritual journal? Have I any record of God's disclosures to me over the past week, month, or year? Am

I learning to recognize them, and in what ways am I gaining in insight? What has been the most "shattering" lesson I have learned in the past year?

WEEK ONE: MONDAY

And Jacob came to a certain place, and stayed there that night, because the sun had set. Taking one of the stones of the place, he put it under his head and lay down in that place to sleep. And he dreamed that there was a ladder set up on the earth, and the top of it reached to heaven; and behold, the angels of God were ascending and descending on it! And behold, the Lord stood above it and said, "I am the Lord, the God of Abraham your father and the God of Isaac; the land on which you lie I will give to you and your descendants; and your descendants shall be like the dust of the earth, and you shall spread abroad to the west and to the east and to the north and to the south; and by you and your descendants shall all the families of the earth bless themselves. Behold, I am with you and will keep you wherever you go, and will bring you back to this land; for I will not leave you until I have done that of which I have spoken to you." Then Jacob awoke from his sleep and said, "Surely the Lord is in this place; and I did not know it." And he was afraid and said, "How awesome is this place! This is none other than the house of God, and this is the gate of heaven." (Gen. 28:11-17)

The Witness of Scripture

Undoubtedly, Jacob is one of the less attractive figures in the record of our salvation history. His very name, by translation, means the one who "over reaches," "supplants," and "beguiles." He had cheated his brother and deceived his old father, and he is now in the process of running away from it all. He is running away from his family, his past, himself, and God. In the process, he takes one of the most godforsaken roads in the geography of the Old Testament. "The track winds through an uneven valley, covered as with gravestones, by large sheets of bare rock; some few here and there standing up like the cromlechs of Druidical monuments" (Stanley, *Sinai and Palestine*).

Clearly, Jacob is not in for a particularly comfortable night's sleep! He is greatly disturbed, yet in that godforsaken place, where he could be forgiven for assuming that he was safe from any divine intervention, "even there also shall thy hand lead me: and thy right hand shall hold me. If I say, Peradventure the darkness shall cover me: then shall my night be turned to day" (Ps. 139:10-11).

For it is in that deserted place that Jacob sees the angels of God restoring the broken communication between earth and heaven: those messengers of reassurance in the very place of despair, those angels of light in the darkness; pillows of comfort among the hard rocks of disturbance and fretful anxiety.

So Jacob might well ask, also in the words of the psalmist: "Whither shall I go then from thy Spirit: or whither shall I go then from thy presence?" (Ps. 139:7). For in the game which most adults play most of their lives—the game of hide and seek—it is the Son of Man who comes "to seek and to save" the lost children of Abraham (Luke 19:10). God's message and God's messengers will search us out, even in the desert of our sin and rebellion, restoring those broken lines of communication between heaven and earth and giving us the reassuring vision and glimpse of the glory and majesty of God's great and abiding love for us. It is a love which, since the dawn of time, has always been ready and willing to go out of its way to seek and to save us.

The Witness of the Saints

SAINT JEROME (ca. 342–420)

Jerome went into the solitude of the desert to study the word of God, and became the greatest biblical scholar of the early church.

Craggy, not at all attractive by nature, brilliant and dangerously clever with words, Jerome was born about the year 342 at Stridon, a small town on the borders of Dalmatia. His father insured that his bright son should be well educated, first at home and only later in Rome, where his tutor was the famous pagan grammarian, Donatus. The young Jerome mastered the Latin and Greek tongues in addition to his own native language of Illyrian. He was baptized in Rome. In 374 he traveled from there to Antioch, where he contracted a fever and nearly died. In his delirium, he saw himself before the judgment seat of Christ. When he was asked who he was, he answered that he was a Christian. "You are lying," was the reply. "You are a Ciceronian; for where your treasure is, there is your heart also." (In other words, Jerome loved the words of Cicero, the great orator of ancient Rome, more than the words of Scripture.)

That was the turning point for Jerome. From then onwards, he sought to direct all his energies and abilities to the study of Scripture. He went to live in a desert monastic community at Chalcis and was subsequently ordained to the priesthood. For a while, he left the desert to study in Constantinople with St. Gregory Nazianzen. From there he went to Rome in the year 382 to act as personal secretary to Pope Damasus.

After the death of Pope Damasus in 384, Jerome felt exiled by the church's leaders, many of whom he had alienated by his harsh outspokenness and sarcastic wit. He felt the need to withdraw again to Antioch, and then later he went to live in a cave in Bethlehem, near the church of the Nativity. It was during these years of retreat and solitude that he wrote his scholarly commentaries on the Scriptures and translated the Scriptures into Latin. It was this translation which was to become the famous Vulgate translation, and which was to be the official Bible for the whole of the Middle Ages. St. Paula, his patron, companion, and monastic friend, died in 404. This was a great blow to Jerome, as was the sacking of Rome, only six years later, by Alaric the Goth.

Somewhat disillusioned, worn out by scholarship, penance, and fasting, Jerome foresaw the coming of the Dark Ages. His sight and voice failing, he died peacefully on September 30, 420. His body was buried first under the church of the Nativity in Bethlehem, and then, long afterwards, it was removed to Rome.

Our Experience

It is in the night time of our lives that the star of revelation can shine most brightly. St. Jerome, like many of the saints, led a difficult life at an especially difficult time in history. Neither Jacob nor Jerome was an especially attractive or impressive character. Of course, the saints are not there to *impress* anybody, because they are generally too busy trying to *express* somebody—Christ who is within them, "the hope of glory" (Col. 1:27). It is only that hope which saves them from despair and ultimate cynicism; for saints are the enlightened ones who are the true lights of the world, yet only in the sense that the moon is a light in the night, with all its light borrowed and reflected from the sun.

Jerome, like Jacob before him, was in danger of sinking into the night of that despair, precisely because both of them alike could have mistaken skill (planning and rhetorical skills) for true gift, cleverness for wisdom, politics for true power, and brilliance for true enlightenment. Yet, we always find all the good news *among* the bad news, and the good news is summarized by St. John: "The light shines in the darkness and the darkness has not overcome it." Nor will it ever overcome it.

So we do not need to fear the darkness of the night, for the Christian looks with confidence to the promise of the Morning Star. We need not fear the darkness of history, for Christ is Lord of history and of the ages (as the paschal candle reminds us each year). However dark the ages may be, Christ is the light of the world for those with eyes to see, enabling us to walk into the darkness with true confidence as we sing ever more insistently, "The Light of Christ." We need not fear the darkness of evening as the "night" of old age draws on, for there especially, Christ our Light, like the pillar of fire for the old Israel and the paschal candle for the new, will lead us through the darkness to that place where he is himself the Sun and the Light. We do not need to be afraid of the darkness—only the darkness of sin and of turning our back on the Light.

For sometimes, it is only in the night of our lives and in the deserted, silent place that God can break through at all to give us the grace of the gift of himself. It is in our dreams and in the space afforded by night, sleep, old age, and retirement—it is in these apparently deserted places of our lives and in those times of apparent uselessness that God "giveth his beloved, in sleep."

So cats are not the only creatures who see in the night! It is the special gift of the saint, who not only can see at night, but also, and equally important, can be seen in the night. Jerome gave to the Dark Ages the light of God's word. To be able to do that for our own age, we do not have to be scholars—only saints!

WEEK ONE: TUESDAY

Now Moses was keeping the flock of his father-in-law, Jethro, the priest of Midian; and he led his flock to the west side of the wilderness, and came to Horeb, the mountain of God. And the angel of the Lord appeared to him in a flame of fire out of the midst of a bush; and he looked, and lo, the bush was burning, yet it was not consumed. And Moses said, "I will turn aside and see this great sight, why the bush is not burnt." When the Lord saw that he turned aside to see, God called to him out of the bush, "Moses, Moses!" And he said, "Here am I." Then he said, "Do not come near; put off your shoes from your feet, for the place on which you are standing is holy ground." And he said, "I am the God of your father, the God of Abraham, the God of Isaac, and the God of Jacob." And Moses hid his face, for he was afraid to look at God. (Exod. 3:1-6)

The Witness of Scripture

Moses had withdrawn from the scene of public life at court where he had been brought up, as a marked man, under possible condemnation for the murder of an Egyptian. He went to that awesome desert area just south of the Dead Sea and spent many years of his life in seclusion, tending sheep and goats for his father-in-law. It was there at Mount Horeb that the one who was "drawn out" (hence, "Moses") from the waters as a child spent many years in reflection in a hidden life. Yet it was in such a place—in fact, the same place as to Elijah—that God granted to Moses his vision. The place of retreat became the place of true education, "drawing out," vision, insight, and self-knowledge.

Moses had long left behind him the political scene at court where he had been brought up, and by his old age, he was thoroughly rusticized—"slow of speech and of a slow tongue," we are told (Exod. 4:10). Yet, by contradiction, paradox, and God's strength alone, Moses was to become one of the greatest political figures of the ancient world, a real "mover and shaker," a leader and a prophet bringing revolutionary changes in the fortunes of his people.

The vision of the burning bush that was burned but not consumed is the first great "theophany" of the Scriptures. As such, it "shows forth" something of the nature of God himself—a God whose love burns without being consumed. Because we are creatures and not the Creator, intense human love is often self-destructive: we are consumed by it, and it leaves us as burned-out cases. That is not so with God. God is a Trinity of Love, Love given and received in love without loss or fatigue. Even at the beginning of his new life, Moses is granted something of the vision of God with its implied ultimate alternatives: "consumed by Fire or by fire" (T.S. Eliot).

It is not accidental that many of the leading figures of the Scriptures received their call to advance when they were in retreat. It is when our natural energies have been consumed by the passing enthusiasms of the years that God can then best use such men and women who have been "fired up" (as we say) by his grace and by the vision of the fire of his love. From a human point of view, Moses, in his eightieth year, tending the flock of Jethro at the "backside" of that godforsaken desert, must have appeared a bit of a "burned-out" case. Yet, he is precisely the kind of old man who can still dream dreams and also see visions.

So, not surprisingly, Moses turns aside to investigate, probe, and look more deeply into the mysterious phenomenon of that burning bush. One of the temptations of old age is to suppose that you have seen it all before, and that there is nothing new under the sun. Such was not the case with Moses. Those years in the desert had heightened his awareness and developed his perception and insight. Such is one of the gifts of the desert with its highly contrasting elements of darkness and light, color, sounds, and silence. It is the place of extremes. It was years of contemplation in that environment that brought Moses to the place of holiness and redirected him into the ways of ministry and leadership. But notice that Moses had first to be delivered and drawn out before he could deliver and draw out others from the bondage of Egypt, through the waters of the Red Sea; through the schooling of the desert to the land of gift and promise.

The Witness of the Saints

SAINT CATHERINE OF SIENA (1347–80)

Catherine of Siena is a case of the contemplative who is up to her eyes in the affairs of the church and the world, but whose eyes are fixed upon the face of Christ. Along with St. Francis of Assisi she is regarded as the patron saint of Italy. The daughter of a wealthy Sienese wool dyer, Caterina Benincasa was one of no less than twenty four or twenty-five children!

At the age of sixteen, she joined the Third Order of St. Dominic, and in so doing opted to go for three years of voluntary, solitary confinement. She never set foot outside except to go to the Dominican church, and she spoke to no one except to her confessor. Her family and friends despaired of her as she pursued with total singlemindedness a life of extreme asceticism, hidden from the world.

Then on Shrove Tuesday, 1366, while she was praying alone in the dark chamber of her seclusion, she was granted a vision which was to change her life radically. We are told that she saw a pageant "incomparably more gorgeous than anything seen on the streets of Siena. Preceded by dazzling light, celestial music with warmth, perfume, color and sheer joy there came towards her the Redeemer, His Blessed Mother, St. John, St. Paul, St. Dominic, David and legions of angels. While the grace and kindly looks of this heavenly

cohort were upon her, with the formality of a betrothal ceremony, she received the eternal assurance of Christ, that, as
she was espoused to Him in faith, his strong support would
never fail her."

This vision totally changed the direction of her life. She
returned to her family, walking straight into the kitchen,
where they were busy eating dinner! Although she only
lived until she was thirty-three, she dramatically influenced
kings and popes. She went—like Moses—before the
pharaohs of church and state of her day and spoke boldly to
them. "Do God's will and mine," she commanded Charles
V. To Pope Gregory XI she said, face to face, "I have heard
that you have created cardinals. I believe it would be more
to the honor of God and better for yourself if you would always take care to choose virtuous men. When the contrary
is done, it is a great insult to God and disaster to Holy
Church. . . . I beseech you to do what you have to do man-
fully and with the fear of God."

She ministered to the poor, to the sick, and to prisoners,
and all the time was up to her eyes in the bitter political in-
trigues of the many Italian states of her day. She traveled extensively on behalf of the papacy and died of a stroke while
praying in St.Peter's, Rome, on the fifth Sunday of Lent,
1380. Towards the end of her life, she dictated to three secre-
taries her book, *The Dialogue*, which is her lasting gift to the
world on the spiritual life.

"Being so closely associated with her," writes Raymond
of Capua, her spiritual adviser, "I was able to see at first
hand how, as soon as she was freed from the occupations in
which she was engaged for the work of souls, at once, one
might almost say by a natural process, her mind was raised
to the things of heaven."

It was precisely what she had experienced in her times
of contemplative prayer that impelled her into action and
concern for this world.

Our Experience

The visionaries are the true activists who, in the end,
make a real difference. Yet, it is those who set out to be ac-

tivists who soon end up becoming the ultimate escapists, and who leave the world in much the same shape as they found it. Again and again in the history of the world, it is men and women much like Moses and Catherine who have first been seized, generally in some seclusion, by a vision, and who have been plunged back into the world—these are the men and women who make all the difference in the world and who bring that world back into the shape of their vision.

Moses was enabled by his vision of God to catch a true vision of himself—"in thy light may we see light." He was turned around and, far from running away from it all, he became even more totally involved in it all. He went back to the scene of struggle and conflict. He went before Pharaoh; he led a labor strike in the brick yards of Egypt and soon found himself up to his eyes in politics, a power struggle, and the leadership of a revolution. So also with Catherine. Her vision totally changed the course and direction of her life. She likewise was impelled to go before kings and popes and to confront the "principalities and powers" of her day and of this world in the name of Christ. Both Moses and Catherine received their marching orders from their vision of God.

Yet Moses was not eloquent. Catherine was a woman. Both found their strength in the One who had made himself known to them through vision, insight, and prayer. It was their times of retreat which enabled them to advance under and in God's direction. It was their times of stillness which powerfully moved them to achieve great things for God. It was their times of silence which gave weight to the words subsequently spoken.

So the true spiritual leader lives a kind of "double life": the larger part of it is a hidden life—"hidden with Christ in God" (Col. 3:3)—and you can't get much more strategically involved than that!

WEEK ONE: WEDNESDAY

When the servant of the man of God rose early in the morning and went out, behold, an army with horses and chariots was round about the city. And the servant said, "Alas, my master! What shall we do?" He said, "Fear not, for those who are with us are more than those who are with them." Then Elisha prayed, and said, "O Lord, I pray thee, open his eyes that he may see." So the Lord opened the eyes of the young man, and he saw; and behold, the mountain was full of horses and chariots of fire round about Elisha. (2 Kings 6:15–17)

The Witness of Scripture

The Bible is the record of our salvation—history as seen through the eyes of faith and perception—what Augustine used to call the "eyes of the heart"—rather than through the eyes that are in our heads.

Clearly Elisha was hard pressed on every side. The king of Syria realized that the prophet Elisha had foresight as well as insight. He knew that Elisha had great powers which were not working in the king's favor, and he was determined to destroy Elisha. So, under cover of night, angels of darkness—the army of the king of Syria—surrounded the city of Dothan, to capture and destroy the prophet the following morning. Next day, the prophet's servant rose early, not to pray, but to prowl! Fear had replaced faith, and in panic the young man looked at the scene of the encamped army, ready to take the city by force. If things were what they seemed to be, there would be no hope for Elisha or, indeed, for his young servant.

Then Elisha prayed. That is the way we should always start God's day if we want to get off on the right foot. He prayed that God would give to his young servant the gift of real vision: not that he would see a different world, but that he would see the same world very differently—from the point of view of reality. The young man's eyes (those eyes of the heart) were opened. What a different scene! He could only see half the truth before, but now he saw things from a

totally different perspective in which confidence had replaced fear, hope had replaced despair, and assured victory
would now replace defeat.

The Witness of the Saints

ST. CONSTANTINE (274 or 278–337)

The son of an emperor father and a saintly mother (He-
lena), Constantine was sent at an early age to the court of
Diocletian, the last and the fiercest emperor to persecute the
Christians.

In 306, Constantine was proclaimed emperor at York in
England. Immediately, he was plunged into war against his
rival Maxentius, whom he roundly defeated at the battle of
Milvian Bridge, over the river Tiber outside the walls of
Rome. Eusebius, the third-century historian, tells us the
riveting story of what happened on the evening of that
strategic battle on which the fate of the empire hung. "Constantine now turned to his father's God in prayer, imploring
God to tell him who He was, and to help him in his present
troubles. It would be hard to believe," Eusebius writes, "if
the Emperor himself had not told me, when I had the honor
to know him, and he swore that this was true. He saw a
cross of light in the sky, and the words, 'In this sign con-
quer.' Night came, and in his sleep, he dreamed that Christ
came with the same sign for him to copy, as a guard against
his enemies. I have myself seen the copy which the gold-
smiths made for the Emperor next morning."

The next day, Constantine roundly defeated Maxentius,
and from that time on, the sign of the cross was used by
Christians everywhere. Constantine's eyes had been
opened, and the authenticity of his "vision" is to be seen in
his subsequent actions. He instigated a genuine "perestroika" in the Roman Empire. Ruling from Constantinople,
his capital city, the new emperor instigated the Peace of
Constantine in 313, establishing Christianity as the official
faith of the Roman Empire, East and West. He encouraged
the church to build great and glorious churches. He wrote to
Eusebius, "Many people are joining the church in the city

which is called by my name. The number of churches must be increased. I ask you to order fifty copies of the Holy Scriptures, to be written legibly on parchment by skilful copyists . . . as quickly as may be. You have authority to use two government carriages to bring the books for me to see. Send one of your deacons with them, and I will pay for them generously."

He humanized the criminal laws and the law of debt of his day and improved slightly the conditions of slavery, making grants available to support poor orphans and thus discouraging the exposure of unwanted babies. In 321, he officially made Sunday the day of rest, and he generously endowed Christian church buildings, especially at the holy sites in the Holy Land. His vision made a real difference to his life and work.

In the Eastern church he is greatly revered as a saint, and has been named the "thirteenth apostle."

Our Experience

It is God alone who can open our eyes to the fuller and larger reality of his world. Most of us, most of the time, are mostly blind. We only see (and generally somewhat selectively) what we want to see, and so often that is only a miserably small part of the whole spectrum of truth, reality, or the larger picture.

In our times of need and in the midst of fear, like Constantine we are driven to look harder, to search and research; to probe more deeply beneath the surface of things to what is hidden from merely superficial observation.

Our prayer life is necessarily, therefore, our hidden life. So Jesus teaches us to go into the inner room, hidden from the world, so that what is discovered, revealed, and made available there will subsequently become clearly evident to the world at large (Matt. 6:6).

God has forces and resources, strength and arms available—but they are all "hidden" beneath the surface of things. We need to go into our prayer "laboratory," that "inner chamber," to see them and to claim them for the battle.

So the real war is within before it is without, and furthermore, it is not so much against the forces of this world, as against the secret forces of evil that always masquerade as angels of light. We need the eyes of discernment that have been trained to see things for what they truly are—for things are not what they seem to be! The battles on the stage of this world are but projections of the larger battles within, beyond, beneath, and above. "There was war in heaven" (Rev. 12:7), of which all the wars on earth are but an echo. In that cosmic battle, all the resources that ensure victory are available to us, if only we have eyes to see them and the grace to make them our own.

But we must remember that we do not seek to enlist the forces of God in our battles, but rather we should lend our weight to the great cosmic battle, in which Christ is our true emperor, captain, lord, and general, where victory is already assured, and where the cross is the sign and standard under which we fight.

So before we begin the battle, each day, in the open field of our everyday life, we will do well to ask the Lord to open our eyes that we may see that fuller picture; that each day we may consciously declare for Christ, and so go in the strength and sure confidence that "those that be with us are more than those that be with them."

WEEK ONE: THURSDAY

And they came to Jericho; and as he was leaving Jericho with his disciples and a great multitude, Bartimaeus, a blind beggar, the son of Timaeus, was sitting by the roadside. And when he heard that it was Jesus of Nazareth, he began to cry out and say, "Jesus, Son of David, have mercy on me!" And many rebuked him, telling him to be silent; but he cried out all the more, "Son of David, have mercy on me!" And Jesus stopped and said, "Call him." And they called the blind man, saying to him, "Take heart; rise, he is calling you." And throwing off his mantle he sprang up and came to Jesus. And Jesus said to him, "What do you want me to do for you?" And the blind man said to him, "Master, let me receive my sight." And

Jesus said to him, "Go your way; your faith has made you well." And immediately he received his sight and followed him on the way. (Mark 10:46–52)

The Witness of Scripture

Situated on a broad, humid plain in the Jordan valley, just nine miles from the Dead Sea, Jericho—the biblical "city of palms"—is now known to be the oldest inhabited city known to humanity.

The city is an oasis, well-watered with springs, and after special excavations in the 1950s, we now know that the earliest habitation at Jericho dates from at least 8000 BC. It is clear from those excavations that the city maintained a large-scale residential community surrounded by massive walls (those walls of Jericho) and stone towers from as early as 7000 BC.

As Jesus was leaving Jericho, surrounded by a great crowd, he encountered the blind beggar, Bartimaeus, sitting by the roadside. The crowd tells the blind man that Jesus of Nazareth is passing by. Yet the blind man is not so blind as he might appear. Perhaps it is the crowd that is blind, because they refer to Jesus simply as "Jesus of Nazareth." The blind man has insight and knows that there is more here than meets the eyes! For Bartimaeus, Jesus is the "Son of David" in that royal line leading to the one who would be the Messiah. The blind man can clearly see what the crowd cannot see.

"Have mercy on me," cries Bartimaeus—the cry of the beggar of the ancient world; *Kyrie eleison*—the cry which the church has rightly taken up in its liturgy ever since.

Jesus calls the blind man to him. Bartimaeus is potentially an eager disciple, for he springs up, we are told, throwing off his mantle, and he comes immediately to Jesus.

Jesus asks the apparently unnecessary question. Yet, Jesus always needs to know what we *really* want. In fact, many still prefer blindness to sight, indifference to a real encounter.

"Master, let me receive my sight," is the prayer for every man, woman, and child; for we are all partially blind, and there is none so blind as those who do not want to see.

So Bartimaeus is given the gift of vision. True vision is a gift of God, given to the pure in heart—the singleminded and those who will one thing (certainly Bartimaeus had that particular quality). "Blessed are the pure in heart, for they shall see God."

His eyes are opened, and the first sight he has is the sight of the Light of the world—the vision of God.

The vision of God is the true end of the human race. Yet, in my beginning is my end. And so, Bartimaeus begins the first day of a life of discipleship, out of the ditch, and following Jesus on the way that leads to eternal life and to the ultimate vision of God.

The Witness of the Saints

DAME JULIAN OF NORWICH (ca. 1342–1423)

"These Revelations were shown to a simple unlearned creature living in this mortal flesh, in the year of our Lord one thousand, three hundred and seventy-three, on the thirteenth day of May."

So begins the second chapter of *The Revelations of Divine Love* by the English mystical writer, whom history calls Dame Julian of Norwich. Little is known about her, yet it is through her that we learn so much about our Lord and his great love for us. History tells us that she probably lived as an anchoress, outside the walls of St. Julian's Church, Norwich, England. She received, according to her own account, fifteen revelations in a state of ecstasy lasting five hours. One other vision followed the next day.

However, *The Revelations of Divine Love* were not committed to writing until some twenty years later. The resulting book, which has gained a renewed popularity in our own age, is the first of her meditations on the original experience, which seems to have consisted chiefly in visions of the passion of Christ and of the Blessed and Holy Trinity. The whole work focuses especially upon the love of God. The writing itself belongs within the English mystical school that flowered in the fourteenth century and which produced the famous work *The Cloud of Unknowing*. In every way, *The Revelations of Divine Love* is a very optimistic work—a very homely spirituality that focuses upon the person of our "courteous Lord," as Dame Julian delights in referring to the second Person of the Trinity.

At the end of the book, she summarizes with great simplicity the substance of all her revelations of God:

"What was our Lord's meaning in it?" And fifteen years after, and more, I answered in ghostly understanding.

"Would'st thou know thy Lord's meaning in this thing? Know it well. Love was his meaning. Who sheweth it thee? Love. Wherefore sheweth he it thee? For love. Hold thou therein. Thou shalt know more in the same, but thou shalt never know other therein, without end."

Thus was I learned, that love is our Lord's meaning. And I saw full surely in this, and in all, that before God made us, he loved us.

In another revelation, Julian contemplates a hazelnut, and makes these observations: "God made it; God loves it and God can take care of it."

Our Experience

The vision that we all need is a glimpse of the reality of God's great love for us. So it is that he longs to show us himself—to show us the shape of love and the cost of love; for the pattern of love is Trinitarian, and the cost and measure of love is the passion of Christ.

But to some extent we are all blind to that love, and there are none so blind as those who are certain that they see it all! Yet, the requirement is not so much that we should see it all, at least not all at once, otherwise we should be blinded—"Teach me as best my soul can bear" (Wesley). Rather, we need to see through it all.

A man that looks on glass
On it may stay his eye;
Or if he pleaseth through it pass
And then the heaven espy.

(George Herbert)

Once we begin to see through it all, there are only two alternatives for us: we shall become either cynics or contemplatives. Contemplatives are, in Shakespeare's language, "God's spies!"

Yet, vision, like true prayer, is a gift, not a talent, a skill, or a technique. It is given first to the people of the first beatitude—the poor in spirit—or, to use the New English Bible translation, those who "know their need of God." The beggar in the ditch, or Julian who knows herself to be "a simple, unlearned creature"—it is to such people (little children, the powerless, and supremely to the poor) that Jesus comes: he opens their eyes to the revelations of his love in the midst of everyday life: in the midst of the ordinary world which is truly, extraordinary and full of God's surprises.

We shall not see his love, however, until we first know our need of his love and can cry with that beggar, and with all Christians through the ages, from the ditch and depths of our hearts, "Lord have mercy, Christ have mercy, Lord have mercy." That prayer will never go unanswered. On the contrary, we shall be continuously surprised by joy.

WEEK ONE: FRIDAY

So Ananias departed and entered the house. And laying his hands on him he said, "Brother Saul, the Lord Jesus who appeared to you on the road by which you came, has sent me that you may regain your sight and be filled with the Holy Spirit." And immediately something like scales fell from his eyes and he regained his sight. Then he rose and was baptized, and took food and was strengthened. (Acts 9:17–19a)

The Witness of Scripture

The light of truth is truly blinding. Yet the good teacher knows that to educate others and draw them out demands one step at a time. Almost certainly, Paul's "education" had been more gradual than the event on the Damascus road, taken in isolation would at first suggest. Paul had observed the stoning and death of Stephen. His excessive reaction against the Christian church was itself perhaps also an indication that he was deeply disturbed and more than usually uncomfortable with what he was beginning to see.

In any event, Ananias had *his* eyes opened that day. Everything was contrary to anything he might have expected if he had relied solely upon secondhand information about this fellow Saul.

Touch is, of course, most reassuring for blind people. Notice how Ananias takes up the role of a good teacher. He is not afraid to touch Paul when he greets him—"laying his hands on him." Secondly, he enters into a relationship with Saul—"brother Saul." Thirdly, he discloses his true credentials: he is there not by choice or on a personal whim, but because he has been sent. Real teaching is, indeed, a vocation after all.

Finally, Ananias ministers to Paul—"speaking the truth in love," as Paul himself was to say many years later. Furthermore, he ministers to Paul's spiritual needs (baptism) and sees to it that he is given food. Both the Sacrament of Baptism and the meal that followed gave strength to Paul.

All these steps are a necessary part of true enlightenment if we are to educate and bring people out of darkness to light, out of death into life.

The Witness of the Saints

SAINT ANGELA MERICI (1474–1540)

St. Angela Merici was the founder of the first teaching order of women to be established in the Western church. Born on March 21, 1474, at the little town of Desenzano on the southwestern shore of Lake Garda in Lombardy, Angela was to lose both parents when she was only ten years old. Together with her other sister and brother, she was brought up by an uncle. Then, when Angela was still only thirteen, she suffered another serious blow: her elder sister, to whom she was very strongly attached, died suddenly before being able to receive the last rites of the church. Angela was deeply distressed for her sister's salvation. Yet it was at this moment of breakdown that God broke through into Angela's life: the same year as the death of her sister occurred, she received her first vision which brought her great comfort and set her mind totally at rest concerning her sister's salvation.

In gratitude, she gave herself totally to God and became, while still very young, a Franciscan tertiary. As such, she followed a life of extreme austerity. The death of her uncle, when she was still only twenty-two, encouraged her to return to Desenzano. She was very small of stature all her life, yet a natural leader. It was not long before she saw the need to start a school for small girls in the neighborhood of Desenzano—indeed, in her visions she saw and perceived many things, so that all kinds of opportunities and challenges opened up for her while she was still quite young.

So successful was the little school at Desenzano that she was soon invited to begin a number of schools in Brescia, and shortly after that she made several pilgrimages, including one to the Holy Land and, in the holy year of 1525, to Rome.

It was during these pilgrimages in 1524–25 that this young woman of visions was struck with blindness. However, during her visit to Rome, she gained a private audience with Pope Clement VII, who suggested that she should stay in Rome to take charge of an order of nursing sisters. She declined this invitation and returned to Brescia, where she was greeted with joy by the citizens, who not only appreciated her charity, but also now venerated her as a prophetess and a saint.

It was about the year 1533, when she was almost sixty, that she began to form a kind of informal novitiate for her teaching companions. The movement spread rapidly. Again, with great perception, Angela saw where her order might go, and so she placed her community under the protection of St. Ursula, the patroness of medieval universities, who was popularly venerated as a leader of women in those days.

So it was that the order of Ursulines was founded on November 25, 1535. At the first election, Angela was chosen as the superior of the community. She died in January 1540 and was canonized in 1807.

Our Experience

Often it is the blows of life—bereavement, disaster, and sickness—that bring us to our knees in times of breakdown. Yet, our breakdown can become God's breakthrough. For sometimes, in order to see what is real and true, we need to know our blindness. Yet, paradoxically, at such times we often cry out aloud, "Oh, now I see!" Of course, what we see in such moments is not a different world—that would indeed be escapism. Rather, we see the same old world very differently, in which things which had been cast down are being raised up, and in which things which had grown old and faded are being made new, colorful, and truly glorious.

We cannot see God's door which stands open for his future for us, until we have found all the other doors to be locked and closed to us; for God's light and his enlightenment at first will always blind us. It is only after we have adjusted our eyes to the light—in other words, changed or repented—that we can begin to see and to know what we should be doing. God can now show us that in ways that we are able to see.

For in that time of "blindness" we are simply compelled to reach out and take hold of another's hand to be led in the right direction. Perhaps Ananias should be called the patron saint of spiritual directors or soul friends, since his hand was available to lead Paul in the darkness of the light which had temporarily dazzled him. Ananias set Paul on the right road, pointing in the right direction. Only so could Paul recover his sight.

St. Angela is, likewise and for similar reasons, suitable to be a teacher—one who educates and leads others, by drawing them through the darkness to the fuller light of Truth. She could do that best, only because she herself had first experienced true education. In her blindness, she was compelled to reach out and to be directed by the one who is not only the Truth, but also the Way. "In thy light may we see light and in thy service find our freedom and our strength."

WEEK ONE: SATURDAY

The next day, as they were on their journey and coming near the city, Peter went up on the housetop to pray, about the sixth hour. And he became hungry and desired something to eat; but while they were preparing it, he fell into a trance and saw the heaven opened, and something descending, like a great sheet, let down by four corners upon the earth. In it were all kinds of animals and reptiles and birds of the air. And there came a voice to him, "Rise, Peter; kill and eat." But Peter said, "No, Lord; for I have never eaten anything that is common or unclean." And the voice came to him again a second time, "What God has cleansed, you must not call common." This happened three times, and the thing was taken up at once to heaven. (Acts 10:9–16)

The Witness of Scripture

Peter is to undergo a complete and radical change of outlook, by the gift of a deep and new insight.

Notice how his bodily hunger and even his environment helped to condition Peter for his vision. He was hungry: his dream involved food. Furthermore, he was on top of the house, on a flat roof, in the seaport of Joppa. He could possibly see the harbor and seaport, with the sailboats passing by. Some commentators on this passage have suggested that what Peter had really seen in his vision was not a "sheet," but in fact the sail of a boat in the harbor. The Greek word *othoné* could certainly be translated "sailcloth," as indeed it is in the New English Bible translation of this passage.

In any event, the curtain between the physical world and the spiritual one is, indeed, a thin one: between dreams and visions; between sacred and secular. Peter's vision confuses him, and so it should, because in one sense it was intended to do so. In the Old Testament, the line of distinction between the secular and the sacred, like that curtain in the temple, had formed a barrier between the two worlds. The new covenant begins as the veil of the temple is torn from top to bottom, and as Christ claims the kingdom of both worlds so that the division might be abolished and all things might come under the sovereign lordship of the one Christ. God *and* man, the Word *and* the flesh, heaven *and* earth—all will now interpenetrate to the mutual enrichment of all. Peter might well be confused, for reality is more complex and not quite so straightforward from now on, either for Peter, for the church, or for the world. From now on, there will be no corner of the secular world where you could ever be quite safe from the invasion of the sacred, for "in His hand are all the corners of the earth!" (Ps. 95:4).

The Witness of the Saints

SAINT HILDEGARD (1098–1179)

A Benedictine nun and visionary of Germany, Hildegard, as a little girl only eight years old, was commended by her parents to the care of Jutta, a recluse, who lived in a cottage near a Benedictine abbey at Diessenberg. At the age of fifteen, Hildegard was clothed as a Benedictine nun, and until she was thirty-two, she led a largely uneventful life, though at the same time a life of intensive study.

It was then that her visions and revelations began, and at the same time, on the death of Sister Jutta, Hildegard became prioress of the little community. Encouraged by her confessor, she reluctantly wrote down her revelations and visions. They were referred to the abbot, Conon, who in turn sent them to the archbishop of Mainz. The archbishop was most favorable in his verdict on the writings, and eventually, after a secretary was provided, Hildegard dictated her principal work, *Knowledge of the Ways of the Lord, or Scivias*, as it was known to the medieval world. This work, divided into three books containing twenty-six visions in all, was promoted by St. Bernard, who commended it heartily to the Cistercian Pope, Eugenius III.

Meanwhile, her community had grown too large for its first convent, and Hildegard was compelled to move her community to Rupertsberg near Bingen, overlooking the Rhine, where she set to work in reforming several other convents and making a special foundation at Eibingen. Like several visionaries, she felt constrained to reprove prelates and rulers and to recall them to the standards of the gospel. Her correspondents included Henry II of England, Emperor Frederick Barbarossa, Pope Eugenius III, and many other temporal and spiritual leaders of her day.

Her learning, writing, and correspondence were prolific by any standards. She was remarkably versatile in many different fields. She wrote poems, hymns, even a morality play, and works on medicine and natural history. In her medical works, she deals with the circulation of the blood, headaches, vapors and giddiness, frenzy, insanity, and obsession. In natural history her writings include studies on the elements, plants, minerals, fishes, trees, birds, quadrupeds, and reptiles. But she was also an artist and a musician. The illustrations which she drew in her principal work, *Scivias*, have recently been reproduced and compared favorably with the work of William Blake.

But it does not end there! She wrote extensively about the importance of sacred music, which she claimed to be "a half-forgotten memory of a primitive state which we have lost since Eden—a symbol of the harmony which Satan has broken, which helps man to build a bridge of holiness between this world and the world of all Beauty and Music." She continues, "Those therefore who without good reason impose silence on churches in which singing in God's honor is wont to be heard, will not deserve to hear the glorious choir of angels that praises the Lord in heaven."

In addition to all this, she wrote several works of theology, including commentaries on the gospels, on the Athanasian Creed, and on the rule of St.Benedict.

She died peacefully, after a formidably industrious life, at the age of nearly eighty, on September 17, 1179. Strangely, attempts to secure her formal canonization in the later Middle Ages were unsuccessful, though she is listed in the Roman martyrology of the fifteenth century, and her cult and name are observed in many dioceses in Germany.

Our Experience

Neither for Peter after his vision at Joppa, nor for Hildegard after her visions, were there any longer two worlds: sacred and secular, holy and profane. The whole world had become for them a sacrament—music, poetry, drama, color, food, sight, and sound; for the Christian professes at every eucharist that "heaven and earth are full of His glory." Our work (liturgy), therefore, as Christians is to break open the glory of the universe and to rededicate and consecrate everything to the greater glory of God, the Creator of all things, for "by Him were *all* things made, and with Him was not anything made that was made." It is one world, and in the end God intends to reclaim it all.

But Christians are not pantheists. The hand of God and his fingerprints are to be found in all creation—on every atom of the universe. But left to itself, the creation does not naturally glorify God. That is romantic nonsense. Because of the sin of the first Adam, creation has been disconnected from its Creator and has sought to glorify itself—mistaking the creature for the Creator (Rom. 1:25).

The work of the Second Adam (Christ) and of all who belong to his family tree (Christians, by baptism and new birth) is to reconnect the creation with its Creator: to consecrate the universe. Only so will the old divisions of sacred and secular, holy and profane, which belong to the old order be replaced in the new partnership of the priesthood of all believers, by "one whole man" who breaks down the "Berlin walls" of the old divisions, claiming "all for Jesus" to the ends of the universe.

Environmentalists, however, so often rely upon a dangerous half-truth: "Leave it to nature by doing what comes naturally!" That will not do. No, it must be nature and nurture working together to bring all things back under the Lordship of Christ: for if Jesus is not Lord of all, he is not really Lord at all! And this is only possible because *all* things are yours, yet only so if "you are Christ's," and all because "Christ is God's" (1 Cor. 3:23).

The Response of Repentance

And I said: Woe is me! For I am lost; For I am a man of unclean lips, and I dwell in the midst of a people of unclean lips; for my eyes have seen the King, the Lord of hosts.

INTRODUCING WEEK TWO

Repentance is the proper response to the gift of vision, and should follow upon it and not precede it. We do not do well if we start with self-examination. First, we need to catch something of the glory and beauty, the love and the patience of God. Then, and only then, in the light of that new insight or outlook, we shall see, in comparison, just how pathetic and shabby our lives and the lives of those with whom we spend our time really are. "Woe is me! For I am lost. For I am a man of unclean lips, and I dwell in the midst of a people of unclean lips: and my eyes have seen!"

The word "repentance" is not a gloomy or negative word. On the contrary—as the saints show us by their lives—it is one of the most dynamic and creative words in the human vocabulary. Repentance—or *metanoia*, in Greek—means to stop and think it out again: to have second thoughts. The wicked old Fagin in the musical *Oliver Twist* sings the enchanting song, "I am reviewing the situation," which concludes with the words, "I think I'll stop and think it out again."

In a word, Fagin is engaged in that most dynamic and creative of all human pursuits—namely, repentance. By limiting the word to an exclusively ecclesiastical context, we have tamed it and taken from it the power to turn and drive us from the negative to the positive, and from looking backward, either with nostalgia or anger, to looking forward with hope, anticipation, and a sense of great expectation.

The saints show us the creative power of repentance as we watch them continually reviewing the situation, sometimes earlier in life and sometimes later.

The saints are the people with truly open minds, who retain the capacity for those second thoughts and for the ability to be surprised. They do not see defeat in the words "I am sorry, I was wrong." Rather, they see the potential for great and joyful victory.

We must all have had the strangely humiliating experience of navigating in a car, perhaps on vacation, or in a strange country. We take a wrong turning. It is not long before the signposts, the scenery, and even our back-seat drivers begin to tell us that we need "to review the situation." In a word, we need to turn around and go back to the fork in the road or to the crossroads and "think it out again." He cannot renew, unless *we* are ready to review!

During 1991, Russia said to the world, in tones which were loud and clear, that they had taken the wrong turning back in 1917. In a word, they repented. That was an essential and (I am sure, for many) a most painful, yet necessary step in any kind of forward-moving perestroika, or renewal, as the word might well be translated.

Repentance gives us, if we will let it, our first taste of resurrection. It tells us that we are in for surprises, for things are not quite all they seem to be at first sight, and that real life is lived back to front. The tomb of death can, indeed, then become for us the womb of new life and new opportunity, if only we see it in the new light of what God can do with all our mistakes. All this depends upon our willingness to repent, to have second thoughts and truly to open our minds afresh to the way that God sees things.

The saints show us how God can change the dark chemistry of our mistakes if we will liberally apply the catalyst of the grace of repentance. The difference is between the night of paranoia and the day of metanoia—the despair of defeat and the blessed hope of eternal victory.

Questions for Personal Reflection or Discussion in Groups

1. Can I find examples of "secular" repentance in history, in the life of a nation, in a biography, or in my own life?
2. What are the obstacles in any culture or educational system to repentance?
3. In what ways do we confuse repentance and guilt, and how can we helpfully differentiate between the two?
4. If repentance is the response to vision, what is the opposite reaction to vision, and in what ways does it show itself in people's behavior?

WEEK TWO: MONDAY

Then Job answered the Lord: "I know that thou canst do all things, and that no purpose of thine can be thwarted. 'Who is this that hides counsel without knowledge?' Therefore I have uttered what I did not understand, things too wonderful for me, which I did not know. 'Hear, and I will speak; I will question you, and you declare to me.' I had heard of thee by the hearing of the ear, but now my eye sees thee; therefore I despise myself, and repent in dust and ashes." (Job 42:1–6)

The Witness of Scripture

There is a direct connection between vision and repentance. We see that connection at the end of the book of Job. "My eye sees thee," says Job, "*therefore* I...repent in dust and ashes."

A new insight leads to a totally different outlook. The bitter misfortunes which Job had experienced led him to paranoia. In the end, there are only two alternatives when we have seen through everything—either paranoia or metanoia. In his paranoia, Job accuses God of dealing with him unjustly. That accusation was based upon hearsay—"I had heard of thee by the hearing of the ear." It was based upon secondhand knowledge. At that stage, Job could not say "I know."

The suffering and the insight brought through suffering had led Job to have second thoughts. Now Job sees that "no purpose" (that is, no detailed plans) of God can ultimately be thwarted. "Job's conversion means that he believed that everything occurring on earth takes place within the framework of the divine wisdom" (John E. Hartley). In other words, God is sovereign and Lord over all his works. It does not mean that God causes evil, but rather that he has chosen to allow evil in order that greater good may come out of it. In a sense, it means that Job's insight has gone very deep indeed, and that he has caught some very small glimpse of the second chapter of God's redemptive plans—which alone could make some sense of Job's innocent suffering.

So, it is Job's vision that has led to second thoughts and to repentance. Without that repentance, Job would have finally committed the sin of spiritual pride. Through repentance, however, he recovers his humility. Pride is a wrong perspective, an inflated view of one's own importance. Humility, on the contrary, cuts us down to size and brings us literally "down to earth" with a bang. We see things in a proper perspective, and so we repent in dust and ashes and the knowledge that we are only creatures and not the Creator—we are successors of Adam, which is translated from the Hebrew as "dust," "dirt," or "of the earth." Humility is the appropriate outlook for creatures of the earth—it is literally "down to earth."

All this leads in the next verse to a restoration of Job's friends, a restoration of his life and his property. Repentance opens the door to a total reordering of our lives.

The Witness of the Saints

SAINT THOMAS AQUINAS (ca. 1225–74)

On the feast of St. Nicholas (December 6), 1273, while he was celebrating Mass, Thomas Aquinas received a special revelation from God that so affected him that he refused to write another word of theology and left his lifetime's work, the *Summa Theologica*, unfinished. "The end of my labors is come," he told Brother Reginald after the special revelation.

"All that I have written appears to be as so much straw after the things that have been revealed to me."

Nevertheless, the church rightly celebrates the life and teaching of St. Thomas Aquinas as the life of one of the greatest theologians of history. From a rich and aristocratic family, Thomas, of "imposing stature, massive build and fresh complexion," was born in the castle of Roccasecca, on a mountain crag dominating the fertile plain of Campagna Felice, overlooking the little town of Aquino in Italy, only a few miles from the famous abbey of Monte Cassino on the road from Rome to Naples. Thomas was taken as a child of five to be schooled at the abbey until he was thirteen. After that, he studied arts and sciences in the nearby university of Naples. During this time, contrary to his family's wishes, he was attracted to the Order of Preachers, and at nineteen, instead of becoming a Benedictine (and possibly a future abbot of Monte Cassino), he was received into the mendicant Order of Preachers as a Dominican. Eventually, after strong and forceful opposition from his family, Thomas was allowed to continue his studies under John the Teutonic, who was lecturing in Cologne. From Cologne, Thomas was called to lecture at Paris, where he eventually received a doctor's chair.

In about 1259, Thomas returned to Italy, where he was made a preacher general, teaching in the school of selected scholars and attached to the papal court. It was in the year 1266 that he began his most famous and written work, the *Summa Theologica*, which was to form the basis of Catholic theology from the thirteenth century until the mid-1960s. Naples was to prove the last scene of his labors. After his special revelation, when he had serious, second thoughts about the whole of his life's work, he was summoned even in his sickness by the Pope to attend the general council at Lyons as theological consultant. He died on his way to the council in the early hours of the morning of March 7, 1274, at the Cistercian monastery of Fossanuova, at the age of fifty. He was canonized in 1323, and his body was translated to the cathedral in Toulouse.

Our Experience

If you have ever had the courage to take out from under the dust of the years those first essays you so proudly produced and presented at school or during your college days, you will hopefully have experienced genuine repentance! In the light of the further reading, richer experiences, and more profound insights of the intervening years, you wonder how you could ever have written such diatribe, and all with such unabashed self-confidence.

Of course, if the Golden Age is in the past, as it was for the pagan world, then you will naturally glorify youth and will regard all the years between as necessarily "downhill." Hopefully, however, the resurrection of Jesus Christ has changed all that for those who have placed their hope in the resurrection and all that it implies. The Golden Age is in the future for us. The witness of humanity and a universe which is running down would suggest that the only prudent thing to do is to "set forth the good wine at the beginning," and then, when people "have drunk freely, that which is not so good." The resurrection has reversed that weary process, of which Cana in Galilee is the glorious first sign. In our dealings with God, at every step along the road, we can keep saying, or indeed singing, "You have kept the best wine until now!" The best is yet to come.

But we can only enter into God's glorious resurrection future through many doors of repentance. "Changed from glory into glory" is the record of Christian experience and Christian pilgrimage. Repentance is the passport into God's future, rescuing us alike from nostalgia and wrong regrets, and giving us the courage to change and to grow— to outgrow our past of this present body and to lay hold of that "new thing" that God wishes to do with us and for us. Remembrance and repentance lead to renewal and resurrection.

WEEK TWO: TUESDAY

But when he came to himself he said, "How many of my father's hired servants have bread enough and to spare, but I perish here with hunger! I will arise and go to my father, and I will say to him, 'Father, I have sinned against heaven and before you; I am no longer worthy to be called your son; treat me as one of your hired servants.'" And he arose and came to his father. But while he was yet at a distance, his father saw him and had compassion, and ran and embraced him and kissed him. And the son said to him, "Father, I have sinned against heaven and before you; I am no longer worthy to be called your son." But the father said to his servants, "Bring quickly the best robe, and put it on him; and put a ring on his hand, and shoes on his feet; and bring the fatted calf and kill it, and let us eat and make merry; for this my son was dead and is alive again; he was lost, and is found." And they began to make merry. (Luke 15:17–24)

The Witness of Scripture

Repentance leads to reconciliation. In the wilderness, eating the leftovers from the swine (an unclean animal for Jews) and with an empty stomach, empty pockets, and no friends, the young prodigal son "comes to himself." Most of the time, we are beside ourselves. Little wonder that we do not know who we are. Suddenly, with a flash of painful insight, he realizes the absurdity of it all. There, back at home, his father sees to it that even the servants get enough to eat. Here, as a son, he is dying of starvation. "To repent is to come to your senses. It is not so much something you do as something that happens. True repentance spends less time looking at the past and saying, 'I'm sorry', than to the future and saying, 'Wow!'" (Frederick Buechner).

Notice the base motive behind the young man's repentance. It does not say that he came to himself because he realized that he loved his father. On the contrary, we are told that he was motivated to return home because his belly was empty. Perhaps God knows that the way to a man's heart is literally through his stomach!

So, back he goes to his father. All the way, he rehearses his three-point speech, with the concluding verse, "Treat me as one of your hired servants."

Yet, once he is in his father's arms, there is no way that he could possibly repeat that third clause. Clearly, he is a son—

yes, a bad son, but he is a son. He could never become a servant. It might make him feel better if he had worked hard enough, and he might have been able to justify himself if he had gone home under those conditions. As the robe is put upon him, and shoes upon his feet, he realizes that he is eternally a son, and will remain a son all his life. It is the steadfast and unconditional love of the father that slowly turns the bad son into a good son and, indeed, into an even better son than the elder boy who had never strayed away from home or stepped out of line. Such is the "economy of repentance."

The Witness of the Saints

SAINT IGNATIUS LOYOLA (1491–1556)

St. Ignatius was a Spaniard, a Basque of Guipuzcoa, the youngest of no less than thirteen children, and from a noble family who lived in the castle of Loyola, near Azpeitia, not far south of the Pyrenees.

As a young man, he showed no signs of being particularly religious. On the contrary, he had distinguished himself as a courtier, a lover, and above all, as a soldier. Indeed, it was the image of himself as a soldier that remained with him all his life, though he was to become a very different kind of soldier—one of the soldiers of Christ.

At the siege of Pamplona, on May 20, 1521, a cannon ball broke his right shin and tore open his left calf. Major surgery (without proper anesthetics) and prolonged convalescence followed. Like Jacob, however, he was to limp for the rest of his life. Yet, it was during that long convalescence that he reached the turning point of his life. On his bed of sickness, he asked for the fashionable romance book of his day—*Amadis of Gaul*. Instead, he was given and found himself reading *Flower of the Saints* and the *Life of Christ* by Ludolph the Carthusian. So it was on second thoughts that his ambition changed radically. Yes, he would be a soldier, but a soldier for Christ. Like an ancient knight, when he was well again, he held an all-night vigil of prayer in the chapel of Our Lady of Montserrat, donating his dagger and sword to the

Black Madonna. He then set out on pilgrimage to the Holy Land. On the way, he came to Manresa and stayed there for ten months, practicing such austerities of fasting and work that his health soon broke down. It was during this time, spent mostly in a cave, that he noted down material for what was to become his famous *Spiritual Exercises.*

After his visit to the Holy Land, he resolved to give himself to serious study. He went from Jerusalem, first to Barcelona and then on to the universities of Alcala and Salamanca. He was imprisoned at Alcala for his earnest spiritual life and for preaching. In both respects he resembled something of an eighteenth-century Methodist! From there, he went to Paris to study for seven years, and it was during this time in Paris that he collected around himself a small band of disciples, of whom St. Francis Xavier was the most famous.

They all decided to go to Rome and put themselves, like good troops, at the disposal of the general—the Pope. On the way, Ignatius had a further vision of Jesus pressing Ignatius to himself and to his cross, with the words, "I wish you to be my servant."

In 1540, Pope Paul III finally accepted the offer made by the newly constituted order to be at the Pope's disposal, and after the vision on the way to Rome, the obvious name for the order was the Society or Company of Jesus. The whole constitution and inspiration for the order was framed in strongly military language: "Whosoever shall wish to bear arms for God in our Society, and to serve only Jesus Christ our Lord, and the Roman Pontiff, His Vicar on earth...." Significantly, the head of the new order was to be called the General.

So it was that the Society of Jesus formed the spearhead of the Counter-Reformation. Missionaries were sent beyond Europe, St. Francis Xavier to India and Japan, and others to China, Brazil, and the Congo. The Society was already famous and the work of St. Ignatius firmly established by his death in 1556.

Our Experience

Repentance, renewal, and resurrection all belong together. When the prodigal son "came to himself," he realized who he truly was: the son of a loving, generous father. Perhaps it is no bad thing that in mid-life many people experience what they like to call an identity crisis—"Who on earth am I?"

The writer Charles Williams speaks of three stages of renewal: the old man, in the old way; the new man in the old way; the new man in the new way. "If anyone is in Christ, he is a new creation," says St. Paul (2 Cor. 5:17). In our baptism we were indeed born again and given a new identity with a new Christian name to match. Perhaps the Christian pilgrimage from baptism to the vision of God is the "time" it takes for the new man in the old way to become the new man in the new way! One thing is certain, namely, that on the way, we take many wrong turnings into dead ends and chase after many fantasies of who we are and where we should be going.

Old Simon was a fisherman, and new Peter will be a "fisherman" also, in a new sense. He will be not so much a fisherman as a fisher of men. Yet, in order to do this, he himself must first be "hooked"! Ignatius Loyola wanted to be a soldier. After his repentance, he would indeed be a soldier, but now he would be a soldier of and for Christ, and not for his own glory, but for the glory of Christ, his true "General," and all for the hastening of the kingdom.

It is significant that the crisis came for Ignatius on his sick bed. It is often true that the crisis (the moment of judgment, reassessment, and "second thoughts") comes when we are laid low; for it is then that we are in the best possible posture to be raised up and given strength that we know is certainly not our own. It was the strength of the Father's love, experienced in real need and deprivation (when the boy was at his lowest), that drew the young prodigal back to his father.

Yet, there is always continuity as well as discontinuity between our old selves and the new self raised up in Christ. Grace does not annihilate nature: rather, it perfects it and transfigures it so that our weaknesses can indeed become our strengths; the pain can become the pearl of great price, and even our wounds are transfigured in a new light to become something beautiful and attractive. The "old man" is transfigured by the chemistry of true repentance to become the glorious new creation in Christ. Thanks be to God who gives us the victory!

WEEK TWO: WEDNESDAY

> He entered Jericho and was passing through. And there was a man named Zacchaeus; he was a chief tax collector, and rich. And he sought to see who Jesus was, but could not, on account of the crowd, because he was small of stature. So he ran on ahead and climbed up into a sycamore tree to see him, for he was to pass that way. And when Jesus came to the place, he looked up and said to him, "Zacchaeus, make haste and come down; for I must stay at your house today." So he made haste, and came down, and received him joyfully. And when they saw it they all murmured, "He has gone in to be the guest of a man who is a sinner." And Zacchaeus stood and said to the Lord, "Behold, Lord, the half of my goods I give to the poor; and if I have defrauded any one of anything, I restore it fourfold." And Jesus said to him, "Today salvation has come to this house, since he also is a son of Abraham. For the Son of man came to seek and to save the lost." (Luke 19:1–10)

The Witness of Scripture

Jericho was known as the city of trees. Jesus was passing through one day when he found Zacchaeus. Zacchaeus was hiding from Jesus, in one of those trees. He wanted to see Jesus, but he did not want Jesus to see him! Zacchaeus did not want to get at all involved with Jesus, but as a collector—a tax collector—he just wanted to add Jesus to his collection. Instead, Jesus was to add Zacchaeus to his collection!

In fact, everything that happened that day in Jericho was a complete turnaround, back to front and upside down. Jesus looked up at little Zacchaeus who had spent all his life being looked down upon. That was how it all began. Jesus asked Zacchaeus if he might stay at his house. Zacchaeus, who had always taken, now wants to give, and in the whole game of hide and seek, Jesus openly admits that he, not Zacchaeus, is doing the looking and the seeking, while Zacchaeus all this time has been hiding. Jesus wins! The crowd is at first amused, then amazed, and finally just angry, because all their expectations have proved false.

The largest block to repentance is our tendency to expect no change. Expecting the unexpected is the prelude to repentance. By sundown that day, life in that city of trees had been turned upside down and would never be quite the same again. I wonder whatever became of Zacchaeus?

The Witness of the Saints

SAINT BRIDGET OF SWEDEN (ca. 1303–73)

The daughter of one of the wealthiest landowners in Sweden, Bridget was married by the time she was only thirteen, and bore no less than eight children, four boys and four girls, one of whom was St. Catherine of Sweden. For some years, Bridget led the life of a feudal lady on her husband's estate at Ulfasa, but in 1335 she was summoned to court to be the principal lady-in-waiting to the king of Sweden's newly wedded queen, Blanche of Namur. The king, Magnus II, was weak and somewhat wicked, while Blanche, the queen, was irresponsible and loved luxury.

Already at this early stage of her life, Bridget was receiving personal revelations, and this became so well known that it became a byword at court: "What was the lady Bridget dreaming about last night?" After several personal and family tragedies, Bridget received leave from court to go with her young husband, Ulf, on a pilgrimage to Compostela. On the way home, Ulf was taken ill, recovered, but shortly after his return he died at the Cistercian monastery of Alvastra in 1344.

Bridget decided to remain at Alvastra for four years, attached to the monastery, living the life of a penitent. Her visions and revelations now became so profuse that she feared delusion. She wisely sought the counsel of a spiritual director, Master Matthias, a canon of Linköping. He was a priest of great experience, learning, and discernment, who helped Bridget to handle the difficult and yet remarkable gift that God had given her.

At this particular time, she received a startling and difficult revelation telling her to go to the royal court and to warn King Magnus of the judgment of God on his sins. This she did, remonstrating with the queen whom she had served so faithfully, and even with the nobles and bishops. For a time, the king responded with genuine repentance and renewal, seeking the reform of his nation and liberally endowing the monastery which Bridget, in the light of further visions, now planned to found at Vadstena, on lake Vättern.

Most of Bridget's prophecies and revelations referred to many of the burning political and religious questions of her day. The word of God for Bridget addressed the leading figures of her time, recalling them to a gospel-centered life. She was courageous in her prophetic remonstrations.

In 1346, she founded the Order of Brigittines at Vadstena, and then in 1349, she went to Rome to obtain confirmation for her order from the Pope. She died in 1373 at the age of seventy. Her daughter, St. Catherine, succeeded her mother as head of the Order of Brigittines.

Our Experience

For us, as for Zacchaeus, putting our house in order is a necessary corollary to inviting Jesus into our lives and hearts. "O come to my heart, Lord Jesus, make room in my heart for thee." For repentance should always lead to a radical reordering of our priorities in order to make space for the things that really matter. In this way, privilege will be transformed into service, as it was for Bridget, and insight will bring about a complete change of outlook.

Notice how the crowd simply cannot believe that Zacchaeus could possibly have had a genuine change of heart. It is the crowd and popular opinion which can hold us back from facing change: "Whatever will people say or think?" We can easily be imprisoned and paralyzed by our fear of what others think about us. Fatalism is a very destructive outlook, because it leaves no room for surprise and thus for the possibility of change and repentance. It would have us believe that what we have been genetically, psychologically, or even astrologically totally determines what we will always be. The popular religion of the crowd lurches between fatalism and superstition, easily giving way to a cynical conservatism to the point of resisting change and renewal at all costs.

Only grace can break through the elemental forces of the universe that condition us and would indeed determine our future, our behavior, or our capacity to change. Bridget's revelations showed her not only what should be, but also what could be. The personal tragedies and disasters in her personal life of position and privilege were now seen in a new light. As problems are solutions in disguise, so also tragedies, seen in the new light of repentance, can even turn out to be blessings in disguise. In effect, the court she served became the court she sought to save. It was those second thoughts born of suffering, grief, and bereavement that enabled her to see her privileges as opportunities and responsibilities challenging her to reorder her own life with new priorities (like Zacchaeus), and to recall others to a reordering of life and to the reformation of society. Yet, notice how the call for repentance comes best from a position of weakness and need, rather than from a position of strength and privilege.

There must be nothing condescending about our call to others to repent. In one sense, Zacchaeus was the very last person in Jericho who could possibly be expected to summon that small-town community to repentance and renewal. And as for Bridget, surely she was too caught up in high society to be able to see that society for what it was. Yet, in both cases, Jesus revealed himself to them, and it is those revelations which led to repentance. Now both Zacchaeus and Bridget saw themselves and the society of their day in a totally new light. Our experience of repentance and renewal demands to be shared with our neighbors, not because we want to put them down, but rather because we long to see them raised up.

Now notice that Zacchaeus was a little man. People had always looked down on him. Yet, in that first encounter with Jesus, the world of Zacchaeus was turned upside down. Luke is at pains to tell us that Jesus "looked up" to Zacchaeus. Surely it was that remarkable inversion and unexpected turnabout that prompted Zacchaeus to come down out of the tree and to see himself and everything else from a new perspective. He had been standing on his tiptoes all his life —climbing up trees and trying to raise himself to advantageous positions. Revelation had made self-elevation redundant. He came down from the tree with genuine second thoughts about everything and everybody.

Low self-esteem is often at the root of sin, pride, ambition, and covetousness. It has taken God in Christ to change all that by "looking up to" us and restoring our image. Jesus comes to us to show us that we are worth too much in God's eyes to settle for anything less than the best.

Bridget is a similar case. Her problem appears at first to be the very opposite of the problem of Zacchaeus, yet both had to learn the same lesson from a different point of view. Both "big" Bridget and "little" Zacchaeus would learn how to become truly great. Bridget was accustomed to high society with the accompanying temptation to look down on others. In her bereavement, she saw that she had relied too much upon the false security that comes from being highly thought of by society. It was in her revelations that she found a new security, because she discovered for herself God's great love for her and how highly God esteemed her in Christ. In so discovering the love of God, she could also preach the judgment of God and bring others to a new outlook upon life, leading even those in high society to genuine repentance. For the love of God and the judgment of God go together. It is not until we know our great worth to God that we can be free to sit lightly to riches, privilege, and high position.

Both small and great, high and low need to know the greater love and the higher esteem in which God in Christ holds them. Only so shall we refuse to settle for too little and the false glitter of worldly esteem. "It would seem that our Lord finds our desires, not too strong, but too weak. We are half-hearted creatures," writes C.S. Lewis, "fooling about with drink and sex and ambition when infinite joy is offered us, like an ignorant child who wants to go on making mud pies in a slum because he cannot imagine what is meant by the offer of a holiday at the sea. We are far too easily pleased" (*The Weight of Glory*).

WEEK TWO: THURSDAY

> Eight days later, his disciples were again in the house, and Thomas was with them. The doors were shut, but Jesus came and stood among them, and said, "Peace be with you." Then he said to Thomas, "Put your finger here, and see my hands; and put out your hand, and place it in my side; do not be faithless, but believing." Thomas answered him, "My Lord and my God!" Jesus said to him, "Have you believed because you have seen me? Blessed are those who have not seen and yet believe." (John 20:26–29)

The Witness of Scripture

It is highly significant that it was Thomas who could not understand the Way, earlier in John's gospel (14:5). He could not see how the terrible, torn body of Jesus that he had observed the previous Friday could now possibly be the glorious body of Christ, as the other apostles reported to him after that first upper room appearance at which Thomas had not been present. Thomas is still reeling from the terrible sight of Calvary and the dreadful wounds inflicted upon Jesus by the nails and the spear. That was his last and lasting memory of what Jesus had looked like. (Often in bereavement, after a dreadful accident or a wasting illness, close friends and loved ones will ask not to see the body, because they want to remember their loved one in the fullness of health.)

Now, in this second appearance, just a week later, Thomas is granted the "sign," and at last he sees the Way that resurrection works. It does not work by suppressing the bad memories and pretending that they were not real. Rather, our memories need to be healed and transformed and transfigured. The wounds and the scars will not go away—they are real enough. The way to deal with them is the way of the nails, by transforming the object of disfigurement into a new beauty, and the shame of the cross (our mistakes, failings, and losses of nerve) into an even greater and more glorious witness. That is the Way, and it is the Way in which Jesus dealt with his wounds and would have us deal with ours.

There is no other religion in the world which encourages an even greater good to come through repentance of evil. It is the Way, the only Way, because it is God's Way of redeeming our world and saving us from our mistakes, our faults, our weaknesses, and our sins. Healing of bad memories opens up to the outlook of a glorious future. We do not have to get it right the first time, but we do need to leave room for those second thoughts!

The Witness of the Saints

SAINT CYPRIAN OF CARTHAGE (ca. 200–258)

"I am a Christian," said Bishop Cyprian to the proconsul Aspasius Paternus, "and only recognize the true God." "Are you obstinate in this determination?" retorted the proconsul. Cyprian answered that such a conviction could never be altered.

But he had not always been so resolute. A pagan and rhetorician, Thascius Caecilianus Cyprianus had been elected bishop only two years after his conversion from paganism (ca. 246). After his conversion, he had studied the Scriptures and the writings of that other North African lawyer and rhetorician, Tertullian. It was only a matter of months after Cyprian had been elected bishop that the Decian persecution broke out, in the autumn of 249. Cyprian chose on that occasion to flee from his diocese and to continue to rule his diocese by letter, until the persecution abated. He was much criticized for this, although he stood firm in his faith at a time when many Christians lapsed and agreed to compromise their faith.

Strangely, Cyprian led the more demanding party in the church who believed that the lapsed should only be allowed to return to the fold of the church after extensive penance and a suitable time of testing. He entered into quite violent correspondence with Pope Stephen. How can a heretic or a lapsed Christian baptize anybody? Surely only an orthodox, professing Christian could baptize another person!

Yet, Rome was steadfast in asserting "that remission of sins can be given by those who themselves are set fast in all kinds of sin"(Cyprian). This discussion occupied the councils of the church in the years between the persecution of Decius and that of the Emperor Valerian in 257. Tradition tells us that Pope Stephen was martyred, and that after Cyprian had gone into hiding, he boldly returned to Carthage and on this second occasion resolutely confessed Christ.

"Are you Thascius Cyprianus?" asked the proconsul at the final interrogation on September 14, 258. "I am," replied Cyprian, on this occasion without hesitation.

"You have put yourself forward as pope of a sacrilegious sect?"

"I have."

"The most sacred Emperor has ordered you to sacrifice."

"I refuse to do so."

"Consider the matter well."

Cyprian had. Now he was clear in his mind: "A matter so plain needs no consideration," said Cyprian with confidence.

The proconsul consulted his assessors and then reluctantly pronounced the verdict.

"Thascius Cyprianus is to be beheaded with the sword."

"Thanks be to God!" replied the bishop. "We will die with him," shouted the Christians.

Our Experience

Many great Christians have lost their nerve at some point along the road of faith and commitment. We know that Peter did so, not only in his denial on Maundy Thursday, but the tradition of "Quo vadis" would have us believe that at the end of his ministry, too, he was tempted to turn back to evade martyrdom. Thomas, the apostle, had craved a kind of certainty of Christ's resurrection which was not wholly in keeping with the way of faith. He wanted to see for himself and to have tangible proofs, after the tragedy of Good Friday (which he had certainly seen for himself), that all was well again. Perhaps a little unfairly, tradition has named him ever since, "doubting Thomas."

For doubt is not the opposite of faith so much as the packaging in which true faith can be uncovered and painstakingly unwrapped. As Frederick Buechner puts it so graphically,

"Doubt is the ants in the pants of faith"! So we must not be afraid of doubt, or try to push it away, as though it were something to be ashamed of for a Christian. Rather, we need to come back again and again to our doubts to reexamine them with second thoughts in the light of newer experiences; we literally need to repent of our doubts not regret them and wish that they would go away. We need to pray to the Lord to give us second thoughts and further insights, for faith is a gift which is readily given to those who ask for it. Then we shall be able to transfer the debit of doubt to the credit of faith, increasing our hope and love in the process.

"Methinks that he protesteth too much" is often our assessment of someone who is just a little too ready to leap to the defense of the Christian faith in glowing words of orthodoxy. It is hard not to suppose that Cyprian was somewhat too hard upon the lapsed in order to compensate for his own timidity in the face of martyrdom. Yet, God knows our weaknesses, as he knew the weakness of Thomas, and will meet us in our weakness and need with that second visitation of reassurance, if we are honest and open about our fears and our doubts. "Lord, I believe, help thou my unbelief."

At his final trial, Bishop Cyprian was ordered to consider his decision by the proconsul. The truth is that he already had: he had had second thoughts long before, and in the light of them he needed no further consideration. Any doubts or fears he may have had were now subsumed in a richer faith which God had given him for this moment, to equip him to witness even to the point of death. We can never be sure, until we are faced with it, that our faith would hold out even unto death. We are all, in that sense, lapsed Christians at some time or another and in some way or another. True repentance will, however, always restore us, for God's love is stronger than all our doubts, and in the end, stronger than death itself.

> Wilt Thou forgive that sin where I begun,
> Which is my sin, though it were done before?
> Wilt Thou forgive those sins, through which I run,
> And do run still: though still I do deplore?
> When Thou hast done, Thou hast not done,
> For I have more.

I have a sin of fear, that when I've spun
    My last thread, I shall perish on the shore,
Swear by Thyself, that at my death Thy Son
    Shall shine as He shines now, and heretofore;
And, having done that, Thou hast done,
        I fear no more.

                      (John Donne)

WEEK TWO: FRIDAY

When they had finished breakfast, Jesus said to Simon Peter, "Simon, son of John, do you love me more than these?" He said to him, "Yes, Lord; you know that I love you." He said to him, "Feed my lambs." A second time he said to him, "Simon, son of John, do you love me?" He said to him, "Yes, Lord; you know that I love you." He said to him, "Tend my sheep." He said to him the third time, "Simon, son of John, do you love me?" Peter was grieved because he said to him the third time, "Do you love me?" And he said to him, "Lord, you know everything; you know that I love you." Jesus said to him, "Feed my sheep. Truly, truly, I say to you, when you were young, you girded yourself and walked where you would; but when you are old, you will stretch out your hands, and another will gird you and carry you where you do not wish to go." (This he said to show by what death he was to glorify God.) And after this he said to him, "Follow me." (John 21:15–19)

The Witness of Scripture

Chapter 21 of John's gospel opens with the old Simon going back to his old ways! Simon says, "I'm going fishing!"

Everything seemed to have gone wrong ever since Caesarea Philippi, when Peter had got hold of the wrong end of the stick about Jesus as Messiah. Everything had come to a head on Maundy Thursday night, when Peter had denied three times that he ever knew Jesus.

Then, after breakfast, as the sun was rising, something began to dawn on Peter. Jesus deliberately sets up a situation where Peter, who had three times denied Christ, might have the opportunity to reaffirm three times—and, in so many words—his love for Christ. Yet, Jesus wishes to press the point home, so that there is no chance this time that Peter will miss the point. Love for Christ must issue in ministry and love for others—"Feed my sheep"—culminating in witness. The old ego in Peter took him where he wanted to go. From now on, his life will "be under new management." He will no longer be in the driver's seat, up front, and if Peter really loves Christ, then he will be ready to follow him all the way, quite literally, so that what has happened to Jesus will one day happen to Peter.

The only hope for the compulsive personality is that life, which has become unmanageable, should finally be brought "under new management." Peter surrenders and discovers true repentance. At the same time, he discovers his true vocation, seen now, not in triumphalistic terms as at Caesarea Philippi, but in terms of patient suffering. Of course, all of this was evident back in the days in Galilee, when Jesus had first said, "Follow me." Sadly, Peter was blinded to all of that in those days. Yet, it had been staring him in the face all the time. Unfortunately, he was too blind to see it. Now, at last, in the light of the resurrection and in the light of the rising, early morning sun, Peter can see the long shadows and the full implications of a vocation to follow the crucified and risen Christ. He will certainly have to stop and think it out again! Walking on water was comparatively easy, compared with all of this!

The Witness of the Saints

SAINT CAMILLUS DE LELLIS (1550—1614)

The wounded physician and one-time compulsive gambler Camillus de Lellis was born in 1550 at Bocchianico in the Abruzzi and by the grace of God became the founder of the Ministers of the Sick.

Born late in the life of his mother, he grew to be a huge man—six feet, six inches tall—and at the age of seventeen went off with his father to fight the Turks. However, he soon developed an incurable disease of the legs, which was to afflict him for the rest of his life. Quarrelsome and difficult in every way, he was thrown out of the hospital for incurables where he went for a time in Rome. For a short time, he returned to active service in the war. However, by the age of twenty-four or so, he had become a compulsive gambler and had gambled away every penny he had earned, all his possessions, and finally, in the streets of Naples, even the proverbial shirt off his back!

He took work as a laborer with the Capuchin fathers at Manfredonia in 1574 and the following year underwent a dramatic conversion. On the feast of Candlemas 1575, the Capuchin father guardian spoke with Camillus about the state of his soul. Ruminating on the priest's words as he rode away on his business, Camillus was suddenly and forcefully struck with the power of the words which he had just heard. He fell from his horse to his knees with tears of repentance. Although he now wished to enter the Capuchin Order as a novice, his diseased leg prevented this, and so he returned to that hospital of St. Giacomo in Rome where he had formerly been such a disagreeable patient. This time, however, he devoted himself as a male nurse to the care of the sick, with such devotion and concern that he became superintendent of the hospital.

In Rome, he placed himself under the spiritual direction and guidance of St. Philip Neri, who was working in the city, and eventually, at the age of thirty-four, Camillus was ordained to the priesthood. He soon founded an order of companions who worked everyday at the great hospital of the Holy Spirit in Rome.

In 1585, living in a larger house for his growing community, Camillus arranged for his congregation of nurses to serve persons infected with the plague, prisoners, and those dying in private houses. Towards the end of the century, some of his companions were sent with the troops on the first recorded kind of "military field ambulance service" to Hungary and Croatia.

St. Camillus, although suffering from serious ill health lived to see the foundation of fifteen houses of his brothers and eight hospitals in Rome, Naples, and farther afield. He was a pioneer in insisting upon fresh air, suitable diets, and the isolation of infectious diseases. In spite of his own serious illnesses and considerable physical suffering, he cared for the sick to the end of his life. He died in Genoa at the age of sixty-four and was canonized the following century. Significantly and rightly, he is patron saint both of nurses and of the sick.

Our Experience

Peter was given the chance to repent of his denial, and to reaffirm his love for Christ and his readiness to serve the Lord and his kingdom. Tradition tells us that Peter was crucified upside down. In any event, he had to learn one way or another to see the whole of life from a different perspective before he could enter upon that real life which is truly eternal.

Back in Caesarea Philippi, Peter had confessed his faith in Jesus as the Christ. He was convinced at Caesarea Philippi, but he was not yet converted (Luke 22:31). At Caesarea Philippi, he had got hold of the wrong end of the stick. For Peter, the Christ was to be Jesus Christ Superstar! Peter's ego was flattered by the opportunity to be "up front" for Jesus. But he did not want to associate with and lend his shoulder to a suffering and, by implication, unsuccessful cause.

Peter thought Christ wanted his strengths and his service, when what God first wants from all of us is our love. It will not be so much our weaknesses that will keep us from the Lord, but rather, much more often, it will be our strengths. We can repent of our weaknesses, mistakes, and sins. It is much more difficult to have second thoughts about our strengths or those talents for which others seem to turn to us, and on which they always seem to be relying. Keeping up the front, saving face, and apparently being in control are all forces which can be so very destructive of faith and trust. Yet, it is by faith and trust alone that we can receive real strength and true gifts.

So the first step in recovering from any compulsive behavior is to acknowledge our need and to be willing to state that our lives have become unmanageable. Yet, for big Peter as for big Camillus, that was a very difficult first step to take. First, they both had to be brought to their knees and to discover their need. In that moment of weakness, God gives us strength and transfigures our weaknesses, turning them to advantage for the kingdom.

"He saved others, himself he cannot save" is always true of those who are saved in and through saving others. True strength is cruciform in shape and contradictory in its dynamics. It is often the big men who are so very sensitive, and who struggle to accept their vulnerability and weakness. So they either become bullies or blessed. "Blessed are those who know their need of God." Jesus wanted Peter to surrender his strengths as Jesus did so dramatically from his arrest in the garden of Gethsemane onwards. Yet, he knew that in order to do this, he would have to turn Peter's life upside down. For our natural weaknesses and scars do not go away—in one sense it is true that the leopard does not change his spots. Instead, our weaknesses and our scars become our true strengths and our stars—but only by grace. The bully in Camillus became the tender, caring nurse. The bragging fisherman in Peter became the faithful apostle. So the compulsive gambler turned on his head and given grace can eventually risk all for Christ. The wounded person is not cured (Camillus' bad legs or Paul's thorn in the flesh were not). Rather, the wounded are truly healed, and in their healing they bring healing to others. Always, Peter and Camillus alike had wanted to impress because of their insecurity. After their conversion, they would certainly make an impression, but no longer by seeking to impress, because now they were too busy trying to express their love for God. That love could now flow more freely because they had first and finally become secure in God's great love for them.

Such insight will have come from many second thoughts, not once, but many times and at many turning points on the journey of faith. All our experiences, good and bad, can serve to bring us to the point where we can even end up thanking God that we are made as we are—that "it is he that hath made us and not we ourselves"—yes, just as we are, weaknesses, scars, and all. "O God I am fearfully and wonderfully made, and you knew exactly what you were doing when you made me as you did" (Ps. 139:14). "By the grace of God I am what I am" (1 Cor. 15:10).

For in the end, true repentance makes regret redundant. *Je ne regrette rien.* I regret *nothing*, because I've repented of *everything!*

WEEK TWO: SATURDAY

"At midday, O king," [said Paul], "I saw on the way a light from heaven, brighter than the sun, shining round me and those who journeyed with me. And when we had all fallen to the ground, I heard a voice saying to me in the Hebrew language, 'Saul, Saul, why do you persecute me? It hurts you to kick against the goads.' And I said, 'Who are you, Lord?' And the Lord said, 'I am Jesus whom you are persecuting. But rise and stand upon your feet; for I have appeared to you for this purpose, to appoint you to serve and bear witness to the things in which you have seen me and to those in which I will appear to you, delivering you from the people and from the Gentiles—to whom I send you to open their eyes, that they may turn from darkness to light and from the power of Satan to God, that they may receive forgiveness of sins and a place among those who are sanctified by faith in me.'

"Wherefore, O King Agrippa, I was not disobedient to the heavenly vision, but declared first to those at Damascus, then at Jerusalem and throughout all the country of Judea, and also to the Gentiles, that they should repent and turn to God and perform deeds worthy of their repentance." (Acts 26:13–20)

The Witness of Scripture

Paul had his eyes opened so that he, in turn, could open the eyes of others (v. 18). It takes a forgiven sinner to convince other sinners of forgiveness. Throughout his whole ministry, Paul's preaching of forgiveness will always stem from his own experience of repentance on the Damascus Road.

It is significant that, after his conversion, Paul went away to Arabia for several years to reflect upon the implications of that Damascus Road vision. When he returned to Jerusalem for his missionary work, his life had been radically reordered, so that he no longer relied upon the law, but rather upon grace, appropriated through faith and upon a righteousness not of his own making, but rather upon that righteousness which is Christ's alone. His "second thoughts" led him no longer to depend upon anything or anybody, except upon "him, upon whom all things depend" (Tillich). Three times in the book of Acts, we hear the story of Paul's Damascus Road experience: once from the pen of Luke and twice from the lips of Paul. Part of repentance is the willingness to witness: to tell your story, not once but many times.

In this third account, the most telling insight was the connection between Saul's persecution of Christians and the persecution of Jesus—"I am Jesus, whom you are persecuting."

Sin wounds God: the knowledge of that should bring us to our knees in repentance. Could it be that Paul's pride had been wounded by his awareness of his sin?

After the dramatic Damascus Road vision, however, Paul can testify that his whole subsequent life had been reshaped and reordered by the vision and by what he came to see as the truth—the terrifying truth! Paul's story sweeps from vision to repentance, to the call to be an apostle, to obedience and self-offering, and even to death and martyrdom.

The Witness of the Saints

SAINT ANTONY OF EGYPT (ca. 251–356)

Driven by the word of God into the solitude of the desert to be tempted and tested, St. Antony was subsequently to conduct an influential and important ministry in the worldwide church. In solitude and armed with the Scriptures, saints are equipped for powerful confrontation with evil in every form.

At a young age, on the death of his wealthy parents, Antony found himself in charge of a considerable fortune and large estates, as well as responsible for the care of his younger sister. During the reading of the gospel at the Mass one day, the words of Christ from the Scriptures spoke directly to him: "Go, sell what you have, and give to the poor." On another similar occasion, the same power of the Scriptures addressed Antony and redirected his life: "Do not be anxious about tomorrow, for tomorrow will be anxious for itself."

So immediately, Antony sold everything and gave his considerable wealth to the poor after first securing a house for his young sister. Then he left for the desert, for solitude, and for the life of a hermit. He fasted and, according to St. Athanasius (his first biographer), he was tempted and assaulted by Satan for many years between 272 and 305, while he lived the life of a solitary and a hermit, first in the desert and latterly on top of a mountain.

At the age of fifty-four, Antony came down from his mountain to found his first monastery. It was not long before there were several others. The monasteries consisted of scattered cells, arranged according to different plans. These monasteries essentially constituted communities of solitaries and hermits, quite unlike the solid communities later envisaged and organized by St. Benedict.

In 311, persecution under the emperor Maximinus broke out, and Antony felt called to go to the city—to Alexandria, to minister to the martyrs in his "white tunic of sheep skin."

The year 355 found him, as a very old man, in Alexandria. By this time, his fame had spread throughout the Christian world. Constantine the Great and his two sons wrote to Antony to ask for his prayers. The saint returned to his hermitage and solitude on Mount Kolzim near the Red Sea; he took his farewell of his monastic brothers and died at the ripe old age of one hundred and five on January 17, 356. Throughout the whole of his life of contemplation and prayer, Antony emphasized again and again the importance of knowing ourselves. His friend and admirer, Athanasius, loved and revered Antony and wrote the first official biography of the saint.

Our Experience

It is extremely difficult for twentieth-century Christians to learn to live in total dependence upon God. In an age of credit cards, it is almost impossible to have the experience of choosing what is literally worth your last penny. This tends to lead us to the point where we do not really know the true value of anything. Repentance involves reordering our priorities, putting at the top of the list the most important things. So often when we do this, we find that our priorities are turned upside down—the first and most important things are precisely those which we would be prepared to spend our last penny on. In other words, when the claims of the kingdom come upon us, they involve us in a whole new scale of values.

So, in all of this what and where is our desert? The geographical desert is, of course, the place where there are no props or substitutes, no crutches, and nothing to protect you from the light, the darkness, the silence, and the solitude. It is as though the desert witnesses to an intensive confrontation with reality—for good or evil. It is, according to Roland Walls, the "primal scriptural symbol of the absence of all human aid and comfort" *(Solitude and Communion)*. Speaking of the Desert Fathers and St. Antony in particular, Thomas Merton comments, "The flight of these men to the desert was neither purely negative nor purely individualistic. They were not rebels against society. True, they were in a certain sense "anarchists," and it will do no harm to think of them in that light. These were men who did not believe in letting themselves be passively guided and ruled by a decadent state and who believed that there was a way of getting along without slavish dependence on accepted, conventional values."

Yet, we witness that slavish dependence at every turn in the road in the twentieth century. It is increasingly common in America today to see businessmen with a mobile telephone perpetually in their hands from morning to night: they probably sleep with one! "Mankind cannot bear very much reality," said T.S. Eliot. We simply cannot bear to be without noise, something to put in our mouths or hold in the grasp of our hands; something to read or something to eat or drink. It is particularly interesting to note, therefore, that when Jesus was training his disciples for mission and evangelism, he told them to take only the bare essentials with them on the road (no stick, no purse, no credit cards, no mobile telephone!). Only so would they experience true freedom and know for the first time the total sufficiency of a life which is lived open to God and totally dependent upon him. All else is, in effect, a substitute. Any and everything else can of course be added as gift and surprise, but "first things first" is indeed the first lesson of the kingdom. We must learn that our first need is to know God and His knowledge of our real needs, even before we ask. This is what is involved in considering the "birds of the air" and the "lilies of the field." And we are "worth more than many sparrows!"

So those early monastic movements were an attempt to give back to Christians the freedom of their birthright as baptized disciples of Jesus Christ. The Desert Fathers attempted to recall worldly Christians, who were looking for a false security in the newly established Peace of Constantine to proper priorities. Once Christianity became an established and accepted religion, it was all too easily seduced by apparent success, prosperity, and the popularity of Vanity Fair. Frequently, these monastic movements literally fled to the desert to recover for themselves the contradiction of a gracious and generous God, who in our poverty will truly enrich our lives; who in our hunger will substantially feed us (but never with fast foods); who in our weakness gives us strength, in the heat shade, in weariness rest and restoration, and in our solitude the continual reassurance of his loving presence.

The Freedom of Forgiveness

Then flew one of the seraphim to me, having in his hand a burning coal which he had taken with tongs from the altar.

INTRODUCING WEEK THREE

"O love that will not let me go" is very much the refrain of the saints, for saints are neither more nor less than forgiven sinners. There is no other raw material with which to make a saint. They are not a special order of being, with special genes that make them particularly good. In fact, the opposite is the case. The worst sinner, by the grace of God, makes for the holiest of saints: those who are forgiven much will love much.

Yet, today, we need to avoid two particular, extreme reactions to sin and forgiveness. We must be neither sentimental about sin nor judgmental. Rather, we need to be totally realistic and practical.

We are generally most judgmental in those areas of our life in which we know ourselves to be weakest and most in danger of falling. We protest too much and feel a little safer if we lash out in a judgmental way against the sins of others.

Equally, we should not be sentimental about sin. It is sin that makes this world the terrible place it is most of the time. It is sin that has robbed us of paradise, and it is sin that is at the root of all the ills of the human race. It was sin that crucified the Son of God.

So, the Christian is just totally realistic about sin and sinners. C.S. Lewis used to say that you could always tell people who did not believe in sins, because they never stopped talking about other people's! It is not, perhaps, quite so surprising, therefore, that our generation, with its gossip columns and its demands for resignation when some political or spiritual leader has fallen, is obsessed with the private lives of our leaders and always ready to hear some smutty story about those in public life.

A realistic assessment of the human condition is never shocked by sins or failings. In the New Testament, Jesus is certainly never shocked by our sins: rather, he is shocked by our fear. We are told in John's Gospel that he "knew what was in man, and needed no one to tell him" (John 2:25). Jesus was able to hold together an utterly realistic assessment of the human condition in which sinners and saints belong together and are held together with the cement of forgiveness. So, we can say of God that as is "his judgment, so is his mercy." God calls a spade a spade and a sinner a sinner, while at the same time, he sees that same person in the light of grace and forgiveness as a saint in the making, already holding a passport for heaven and for the community of worship and grace.

So you will find that saints are the very opposite of most of us, most of the time. They are very strict and severe with themselves, but always generous and lenient with others. They are not too quick to say what is good for others, because they are rightly first concerned with what is best for themselves.

The glorious freedom of being a Christian is that you do not have to win. You can afford to be a good loser. Is there anything more tedious than the little boy who cannot bear to lose a game of chess? Either he kicks the board over halfway through the game, or he tries to change the rules so that he ends up winning the game. We call it situational ethics!

No—the Christian needs to have recourse to none of these ways. The Christian can afford to lose, many times, because Christ has won, once for all. That is the glorious good news of the gospel, which we see in the joy and glory of the saints of God and which we need to recover and reclaim for our generation.

> Plenteous grace with thee is found,
>   Grace to cover all my sin;

Let the healing streams abound
    Make and keep me pure within.

(Charles Wesley)

Questions for Personal Reflection or Discussion in Groups

1. Am I aware of someone I still need to forgive, or someone whom I need to ask for forgiveness? Could it be that this constitutes a "roadblock" in the way of personal renewal and growth in faith?
2. Under what circumstances could we suppose that God would withhold his forgiveness?
3. Have I ever availed myself of the Sacrament of Reconciliation? Are there certain circumstances under which I should use this gospel sacrament of reassurance?

WEEK THREE: MONDAY

Jesus said, "You have heard that it was said, 'You shall love your neighbor and hate your enemy.' But I say to you, Love your enemies and pray for those who persecute you, so that you may be sons of your Father who is in heaven; for he makes his sun rise on the evil and on the good, and sends rain on the just and on the unjust. For if you love those who love you, what reward have you? Do not even the tax collectors do the same? And if you salute only your brethren, what more are you doing than others? Do not even the Gentiles do the same? You, therefore, must be perfect, as your heavenly Father is perfect." (Matt. 5:43–48)

The Witness of Scripture

There can be little doubt that Matthew's gospel was written primarily for Jewish readers, for whom the primary question would necessarily be, "In what ways do the Law and the Old Testament relate to Jesus, and what is the relationship of his life and teaching in the New Testament to all that goes before him in the Old?" Matthew addresses that question from cover to cover in his gospel and nowhere more so than in the Sermon on the Mount in chapters 5, 6 and 7 of his gospel.

The Sermon on the Mount, beginning with the beatitudes, is intended to parallel the giving of the Law of Moses on the mountain of God in the Old Testament. The refrain is frequently used, "It was said...but, I say to you." In all of this, Jesus is not abolishing the Law, but rather he is fulfilling it and even going beyond it. This is especially true in his teaching about forgiveness. The Old Testament teaches atonement through the undertaking of sacrifices and other details of the Law. The New Testament goes further—that "second-mile" kind of loving that transcends the Law. Infinite, unconditional forgiveness is available for the asking. It cannot be earned, but can only be freely given by God who is more than a judge and Creator—he is now the most loving Father.

Yet, as the law in the Old Testament cuts both ways, horizontal and vertical, such is also the case in the New Testament. Those who can receive infinite, unconditional forgiveness from a heavenly Father must be ready to give that same forgiveness to their brothers and sisters on earth— even to those who are their enemies. This is some of the most radical and revolutionary teaching of Jesus, and, if we took him at his word, it would make the church once again, overnight, the most radical and revolutionary force in the world today.

The Witness of the Saints

SAINT ALPHEGE (954–1012)

After entering the monastery of Deerhurst in Gloucestershire as a young man, Alphege became abbot of the monastery at Bath at quite an early age. At the death of Ethelwold, bishop of Winchester, the aging archbishop Dunstan, of Canterbury prevailed heavily upon Alphege to accept the vacant see of Winchester. Alphege, who was only thirty years old at the time, was strongly opposed to becoming a bishop. However, Dunstan refused to take no for an answer, and so a somewhat reluctant Alphege became bishop of Winchester in 984.

During his episcopate, he became famous both for his extreme discipline of fasting and also for his great care for the poor. One chronicler tells us that he became so thin during his prolonged periods of fasting that people claimed to be able to see through his uplifted hands at Mass! We are also told that his care for the poor was so effective that during his time as bishop of Winchester, beggars disappeared from his diocese.

He remained bishop of Winchester for twenty-two years, after which he was translated to Canterbury as archbishop in succession to Aelfric. Throughout the whole of this period, Anglo-Saxon England was suffering from the ravages and continuous raids of the Danes. In 1011, the Danes laid seige to the city of Canterbury. Although many people offered to help Archbishop Alphege to escape from the city during the siege, he refused to leave his people or his diocese. The city was finally taken by the Danes, who slaughtered hundreds of citizens, old and young, men and women alike. The archbishop pressed through the crowds and the carnage to plead with the Danes for his people. He was immediately seized and imprisoned for several months. During his imprisonment, we are told that he healed many Danes who were dying in great numbers during an epidemic which broke out at that time. Furthermore, the saintly archbishop prayed with the diseased, giving them blessed bread. Many of them were healed at his hands.

Nevertheless, the Danes refused to release their hostage unless the country paid a large ransom of some three thousand golden crowns for his release. The archbishop was adamant that his country was far too poor to pay such a ransom. So it was that he was taken from Canterbury to Greenwich on the River Thames in London, and upon a second refusal to pay the ransom, he was pelted with ox bones by the furious and drunken barbarians. Despite a heroic attempt to save the archbishop by Thorkell the Tall, he was finally killed by a blow on the head with an axe.

After his death, his body was recovered and buried in

St. Paul's Cathedral, London. In 1023, the Danish King Canute ordered that his body should be laid to rest in Canterbury.

Our Experience

Forgiveness is the most revolutionary force available to humanity. It radically reverses the whole chemistry of self-destruction in the universe with a force and power for new creativity. Giving back what you get in the equation of "an eye for an eye" leaves the whole universe exactly as it was before. The work of Christ and of his people is to put love back into the universe where there was no love before. Merely loving those who love us will achieve nothing: we are simply parasites. Christians are called upon to change the world and not simply to maintain the status quo.

Yet, of course you will rightly ask, "But where on earth is this extra love—this second-mile loving—to come from?" The answer is, of course, from nowhere else except from God himself, via Calvary on that darkest of days, when the first word to be heard from that cross was not a curse, but a blessing: "Father, forgive them for they do not even know what they are doing."

So the Christian is not concerned with likes and dislikes, feelings and preferences. The objective reality and resource upon which we draw for this kind of loving is not so much our love for others as God's love for all. As we look our enemy in the face, we need to recall that God loves him or her just as much as he loves us, and that Christ died for all. That is the objective reality, or the bottom line, as we like to say, which underscores all our ephemeral feelings, emotions, loves, and hates. "God loves you, even you, damn it—even if I hate you."

Then, from that point of blunt honesty, you can move on to forgiveness. How is God able to love such a loathsome person as I know my neighbor to be? The answer is, quite simply, that God loves all without exception, otherwise how on earth could I ever be sure that he could love me? I am relying upon the fact that God has forgiven me, and I certainly know that I have done nothing to deserve that. God has forgiven me my debt. All my life and for eternity I shall be eternally indebted. In all honesty, therefore, I cannot go out and withhold forgiveness to another just because they do not deserve it. In any case, forgiveness is not mine to give or withhold. It has been bought at a great price and given away freely right across the board.

Perhaps now we can see where the forgiveness that Alphege gave to those who imprisoned and finally murdered him came from: for in truth it was not so much *his* forgiveness as God's forgiveness that Alphege offered to them. The prayer of the kingdom is quite explicit: "Forgive us our sins and debts as we forgive those who sin against us." It is going to have to be that way, otherwise no one would qualify for heaven. People in glass houses simply cannot afford to throw stones!

Of course, none of this is fair, because it goes much further than just doling out to each what he or she deserves. Thank God I do not get what I deserve. It ill befits me, therefore, to begin calling upon justice when I know that straight justice would have condemned me long ago. For if God "would be extreme to mark what is done amiss, then who 'indeed' may abide it?" (Ps. 130:3)

WEEK THREE: TUESDAY

"Come, let us return to the Lord; for he has torn, that he may heal us; he has stricken, and he will bind us up. After two days he will revive us; on the third day he will raise us up, that we may live before him. Let us know, let us press on to know the Lord; his going forth is sure as the dawn; he will come to us as the showers, as the spring rains that water the earth." (Hos. 6:1–3)

The Witness of Scripture

"Let us press on to know the Lord" might well be the subtitle for the book of the prophet Hosea. Written in the eighth century before Christ, during the prosperous and peaceful years of Jeroboam II, the prophet Hosea challenges the unfaithfulness of Israel to Yahweh, and likens it to the unfaithfulness of an adulteress.

However, while the book of Hosea was written at a time when the northern kingdom of Israel was under the shadow of annihilation by the rising Assyrian empire, it is also one of the most tender prophetic books in the Old Testament. Hosea parallels the unfaithfulness of Israel in worshiping other gods, with the unfaithfulness of Gomer, an adulteress —Hosea's wife and possibly a temple prostitute. In chapter 11 and in this passage we see a tender, loving, and forgiving God who is ready to draw Israel back to himself "with the bands of love" (11:4) and to forgive the "prostitution" of Israel, as Hosea is asked to forgive Gomer and to take her back as his wife.

The insight of this prophetic book is remarkable, coming as it does eight centuries before Christ. In a word, the message of Hosea is one of reassurance and hope, even for sinners, and marks the beginning of that insight in religion which was finally to be manifested as the love of God revealed in the face of Christ Jesus.

The Witness of the Saints

JOHN WESLEY (1703–91)

"In the evening" (May 24, 1738), wrote John Wesley in his *Journal*, "I went very unwillingly to a society in Aldersgate Street, where one was reading Luther's preface to the epistle to the Romans. About a quarter before nine, while he was describing the change which God works in the heart through faith in Christ, I felt my heart strangely warmed. I felt I did trust in Christ, Christ alone for salvation; and an assurance was given me that He had taken away my sins, even mine, and saved me from the law of sin and death."

Such was the great turning point in the life of John Wesley—ordained priest in the Church of England in 1725, missionary in Georgia, USA, and founder of the Methodist Renewal movement.

Although he remained a member of the Church of England to his death at the ripe age of eighty-eight years, he was gradually alienated from the institutional structures of that church, as his movement for spiritual renewal and personal faith grew and developed, not only in England but also in America and Europe. Finding the doors and pulpits of the established church closed to him, he took to field preaching, organizing a body of lay pastors to follow up his fervent evangelization. His annual journeyings averaged eight thousand miles on horseback. He wrote thousands of letters and preached sermons without number. Wesley was consistent in wishing that the renewal movement should take place within the structures of the church, and he earnestly hoped that it would be accepted by the established church. However, as the need for ordained ministers, especially in America, emerged, he finally decided that he himself would ordain certain superintendents or bishops. In this way, the movement broke away from the Church of England.

Undoubtedly, Wesley was one of the greatest figures in a great age of reawakening. Along with his brother Charles, who wrote so many hymns that are beloved to this day, he influenced other spiritual leaders of his age—such people as William Wilberforce, John Newton, George Whitfield, Hannah More, and many others who, in turn, changed the whole direction of English society. As a powerful evangelist, Wesley sought with an ardent passion that colored his preaching at all times to bring to others (especially outside the church) that saving knowledge of God's love and forgiveness which had been so formative in his own Christian discipleship. A brilliant intellect, he nevertheless opened his heart also to the power of the gospel, and it was this "double grip" of heart and mind, theology and experience, administration and pastoral flare which gave fire to the evangelical revival that so strongly influenced and colored the eighteenth century.

Our Experience

The assurance of sins forgiven is the birthright of every baptized Christian who has been born again. The heart of the gospel is not, however, "I'm O.K. You're O.K. and therefore it's O.K." because it clearly isn't! (Otherwise what's he doing nailed to that tree?) To start with, I am certainly not O.K. and you would only have to live with me for twenty-four hours to know just how very "un-O.K." I really am!

No, the heart of the gospel is quite other: in fact, it is the very opposite. It could read something like this, I suppose: "I am not O.K. You are not O.K. But thanks be to God, he has made it O.K." So the Christian is in every sense a walking contradiction—clearly and obviously a sinner, yet justified and reckoned righteous. It is precisely because of my baptism that God has chosen to see me in a new light. God has chosen to look at me, no longer in my naked humanity which is clearly so sinful and abhorrent to an all-holy God, but, rather, clothed in the likeness of Christ, his sinless, beloved Son. At Christ's baptism, God said once and for all to Jesus the same words that he says to me in my baptism: "You are my beloved Son, and you are a true delight to me." So "look not on us, but look on us as found in Him," we sing in the great eucharistic hymn.

    Faith is the affirmation and the act,
    Which binds eternal truth to present fact.
                                        (Coleridge)

The present fact is that daily I am clearly a sinner, yet God has chosen to hold together and bind together by faith that eternal truth with the present fact—"making one new, whole person." (Eph. 2:15). So the eternal truth and the good news which we all need to discover for ourselves is that God loves me; Christ died for me; I am a forgiven sinner and yes, in the end, it really is O.K.

All the sacraments are extensions of the one great sacrament of reassurance—namely, baptism. I cannot renew my baptismal vows, because my baptismal status, unlike my driver's license, will never run out! Nevertheless, I will need again and again to reaffirm my baptismal status. There are all kinds of ways of doing this. Some Christians find the practice of using holy water at the entrance to the church a helpful reminder of who they are and whose they are, as they go before the Lord in prayer and worship. (The sign of the cross with water as at baptism is an action that speaks louder than words but which can say the same thing—namely, "It's O.K.") Others find that kneeling before a crucifix in the Sacrament of Reconciliation can bring a reassurance that they are truly forgiven. (Indeed, the prayer book of 1662 tells us that we should do just that if we cannot find the reassurance of

sins forgiven any other way.) We are not earning any other
forgiveness than that which is already ours from Calvary
and through baptism. Rather, we are recalling that forgiveness once and for all in the light of our sins and failings and
by hearing the priest proclaim the gospel words, "Go in
peace—it really is O.K., and you need to know it!"

Many Christians are accustomed to placing the paschal
candle of Easter and baptism next to the coffin or burial cas-
ket at the funeral of a Christian. It reassures them that however dark the passage of death may be, in the light of their
baptism and Christ's death, even in the valley of the shadow
of death, "it's O.K."—with thee, dear Lord, beside me; Thy
rod and staff me comfort still, thy cross before to guide me."

All this was Wesley's experience at the turning point of
his life in Aldersgate. For too long he had treated his Christian faith as *his* insurance policy. Then on that special evening, at last he discovered for himself what every baptized
Christian needs to know. The Christian life is not *my* insurance policy, but rather *God's* new insurance policy on which
he has paid the premium and which he has drawn up specially for fearful Christians like John Wesley who need a living
faith in a God who knows all and has chosen to forgive all.

WEEK THREE: WEDNESDAY

And Jesus answering said to him, "Simon, I have something to say to you." And he answered, "What is it, Teacher?" "A certain creditor had two debtors; one owed five
hundred denarii, and the other fifty. When they could not
pay, he forgave them both. Now, which of them will love
him more?" Simon answered, "The one, I suppose, to
whom he forgave more." And he said to him, "You have
judged rightly." Then turning toward the woman he said
to Simon, "Do you see this woman? I entered your house,
you gave me no water for my feet, but she has wet my
feet with her tears and wiped them with her hair. You
gave me no kiss, but from the time I came in she has not
ceased to kiss my feet. You did not anoint my head with
oil, but she has anointed my feet with ointment. Therefore
I tell you, her sins, which are many, are forgiven, for she

loved much; but he who is forgiven little, loves little." And he said to her, "Your sins are forgiven." Then those who were at table with him began to say among themselves, "Who is this, who even forgives sins?" And he said to the woman, "Your faith has saved you; go in peace." (Luke 7:40–50)

The Witness of Scripture

Luke, the only Gentile author in the New Testament, brings a particular perspective to the eternal gospel of Jesus Christ. Generally supposed to have been "Luke, the beloved physician" of Paul's acquaintance and the author of Acts, he gives glimpses of medical interest in his writings. Women, too, have a particularly pronounced place in his gospel. But, above all, it is Luke's emphasis upon a forgiving God which stands out most clearly throughout the two volumes of his writings. After all, it is to Luke that we owe the record of the two most famous parables of Jesus—namely, the Good Samaritan and the Prodigal Son. It is only in Luke that we are told that the "Lord turned and looked at Peter" as the cock crowed during the trial of Jesus, after Peter had denied his friendship with the Lord. Finally, it is to Luke that we owe the record of the first words from the cross: "Father, forgive...."

Although the story of the prostitute anointing Jesus is found in all the gospel traditions of the New Testament in one form or another, it is only in Luke that we have the story of the forgiven debtors inserted as a story within the story. In the inner story, we have the most articulate development of the economy of forgiveness to be found anywhere in the gospels. The story draws together the double implications—vertical and horizontal—of God's forgiveness. You cannot earn forgiveness, but you must be ready to give the most precious gift of forgiveness to others in the same generous way as you have received it: "Forgive us our debts, as we forgive the debts of others" is the ultimate economy of the kingdom.

Furthermore, the formula of the relationship between love and forgiveness opens up the door to a brave new world of holiness and godliness which is to the old world order of virtue what technicolor is to black and white. The saints glow with the glory of forgiveness.

The Witness of the Saints

SAINT AUGUSTINE OF HIPPO (354–430)

"Too late have I loved you, Beauty so old and so new! Too late have I loved you. And behold, you were within me and I was caught up in the external world and it was there that I searched for you, deformed, plunging, absorbed in those beautiful forms which you had made. You were with me, but I was not with you. The lovely things kept me far from you—things which would not have existed at all except for you. You called, you shouted, and burst in on my deafness. You flared into light and were resplendent, you put to flight my blindness. You breathed forth fragrances and I drew in my breath and now I pant after you. I tasted you and still I feel hunger and thirst for you. You touched me, and now I burn with desire for the peace which is your gift" (*Confessions* 10, xxvii 38).

Augustine of Hippo was converted dramatically at the age of thirty-two and was subsequently baptized the following year (387) at the hands of Bishop Ambrose of Milan, together with Alypius, Augustine's closest friend, and Adeodatus, Augustine's illegitimate son. The first part of Augustine's life had been consumed with ambition, lust, and preoccupation with self, though, as he tells us in his *Confessions*, from an early age he had a strong sense of God and was deeply religious, almost to the point of obsession. He spent the early years of his life shopping around the extensive supermarket of religious options available towards the twilight years of the Roman Empire.

Tolle, lege: tolle, lege, said the voice of what Augustine first thought to be that of a little girl playing in the neighboring garden on that hot summer's afternoon in 386. "Pick it up and read it; pick it up and read it." So he did. He picked up a copy of St. Paul's epistles which happened to be lying on the ground nearby. There and then in that garden in Milan the book fell open at the tenth chapter of Paul's epistle to the Romans. The words leapt from the page and spoke directly to Augustine's heart. "Not in revelling and drunkenness, not in debauchery and licentiousness...but put on the Lord

Jesus Christ." So it was that there and then, Jesus Christ saved Augustine from the darkness of his sins and his religiosity and brought him into the light of the gospel of reconciliation, healing, and peace.

Originally from North Africa, to North Africa he would return, together with Adeodatus and Alypius. Sadly, his mother Monica, whose prayers and tears of intercession since Augustine's earliest childhood had, humanly speaking, brought about Augustine's conversion, died in Ostia, the port of Rome, while the whole family party was waiting for a ship to take them back to their native country.

Once home, Augustine set up a community and led an austere life of study and prayer in the fellowship of the gospel. Very shortly after his arrival, he was ordained priest, and subsequently, within the short span of five years, he was to become bishop of Hippo—today Anaba, on the north coast of Algeria. So it was that he was to spend the rest of his long life (he died in 430 at the age of seventy-six) as a teaching, preaching, and writing bishop. He wrote many works of theology; he defended the orthodox faith in the frequent councils in Carthage; he opposed heretics—from the successful but graceless Donatists to the smooth and plausible Pelagius—and in his own day and over the centuries since, he has become—perhaps second only to St. Paul—the most formative single voice for gospel Christianity in the history of the Western church.

Augustine was under no illusions. He knew that he owed his salvation and his conversion to grace and to grace alone. Through all his theological presentations and writings, the constant theme is always the primacy of that grace and God's initiative in all things, from start to finish. He died after a long life that witnessed in every chapter and on every page to the power of God's grace and love in all things. "Love God and do as you like," when properly understood encapsulates the message and the life of this passionate apostle of Jesus Christ. Except for his right arm, which is still in a reliquary in the great church of St. Augustine in Hippo, the rest of his body, bought for the equivalent of its weight in gold, rests today in the Augustinian church in Pavia, Italy. His influence has lived on since the fifth century, especially through the writers of the Reformation period, and also through all serious thinkers and students of Western civilization down to our own day.

Our Experience

St. Augustine was supremely the apostle of grace, forgiveness, and love. He loved much and was forgiven much. Yet, forgiveness can never put the clock back. For humanity there is no going back to the innocence of the Garden of Eden and all that. The only option open to repentant sinners is sanctity and holiness. Any married couple knows that after a row, half the fun is "making up," because things cannot go back to where they were: if they are to go forward, they must go deeper.

According to the epistle to the Hebrews, Adam and Eve were created "a little lower than the angels." Yet, redeemed and forgiven humanity in Christ is now above the angels. The medieval carol celebrates this remarkable reversal in extravagant language: "Nay had the apple taken been/Our Lady ne'er been heavenly Queen....So blessed be the time that apple taken was!"

God's plan for our redemption is too hot to handle. Saint Augustine cannot refrain from equally paradoxical language when he insists upon saying *O felix culpa*—"O happy sin." Where on earth is all this leading? you might well ask. Of course, it is not leading anywhere on earth at all, either to the garden of Eden or to the desert of sin. In the end, it is leading straight to heaven, where, you remember, there is more rejoicing over one sinner who repents than over ninety-and-nine just persons who have no need of repentance. As the argument develops, you might well ask, "So, shall we sin more that grace may abound?" No, God forbid! Yet, this glorious formula for our redemption, the gospel itself in all its richness and the life and witness of Augustine, constitute the kind of hot potato that the church, let alone the world, has scarcely ever been able to handle. Our church, today especially, needs to recover this powerful doctrine of salvation, for the test of the Christian church is not so much whether it can make good men and women better, but rather whether it can make bad men and women holy.

Looking ahead, we must always seek to avoid sin. It is a terrible thing: it crucified the Son of God. Yet, at the same time and in retrospect, when we have sinned and repented, to be forgiven is more wonderful than if we had not sinned in the first place. Such a strategy for salvation is widely open to abuse. It is reflected in the formula for health in the human body. Health after disease is even greater than before the illness, if the body has itself been able to produce the antibodies to the disease. Put another way: the door through which sin enters life can be like the butler's door that swings both ways. The door through which the dirty, empty dishes are taken from the table is the same door through which the good food of the next course enters. It is as though repentance is a no-lose situation!

Little wonder that Augustine, who had grasped the full catholic doctrine of salvation (or rather, had been grasped by it), should have fallen neither for the Donatist heresy that would lead to perfectionism, nor for the plausible platitudes of the smooth Pelagius. Augustine knew from his own experience, as Paul before him and millions of forgiven sinners have known after him, that God's grace is indeed sufficient for any and all sin, and that the key which unlocks the final door into heaven is cruciform in shape and manufactured from the nails used at Calvary. In a word, we are ultimately justified by grace—amazing grace—and grace alone! That is not only good news, it is the best news going anywhere in the universe. Salvation is far better than restoration, and the saints testify to that in their lives.

> Amazing Grace! How sweet the sound
> That saved a wretch like me.
> I once was lost; but now am found;
> Was blind, but now I see.
>   (John Newton)

WEEK THREE: THURSDAY

Jesus said, "Two men went up into the temple to pray, one a Pharisee and the other a tax collector. The Pharisee stood and prayed thus with himself, 'God, I thank thee

that I am not like other men, extortioners, unjust, adulter-
ers, or even like this tax collector. I fast twice a week, I
give tithes of all that I get.' But the tax collector, standing
far off, would not even lift up his eyes to heaven, but beat
his breast, saying, 'God, be merciful to me a sinner!' I tell
you, this man went down to his house justified rather
than the other; for every one who exalts himself will be
humbled, but he who humbles himself will be exalted."
(Luke 18:10–14)

The Witness of Scripture

We must realize that, in so many ways, the Pharisees
were the most virtuous people in the whole of Israel. There
would never be more than about six thousand of them in Israel at any one time, belonging as they did to a kind of
brotherhood known as the Chaburah. They would be initiated
into this brotherhood in the presence of three witnesses as
into a kind of "moral freemasonry," and they would solemnly
pledge to spend their whole life observing every detail of
the scribal Law. The name Pharisee means "the separated
one," and as such, the Pharisee would pursue a very remarkable and indeed estimable lifestyle, fasting two days
each week, tithing his income to the synagogue, and caring
for the poor through the considerable ministry to the poor
which every synagogue undertook. We should not underes-
timate the virtue of the Pharisees.

Tax collectors were, on the other hand, extortioners, unjust and disloyal to their country. Not surprisingly, they
were hated by all and respected by neither their fellow Jews
whom they oppressed, nor by the Romans to whom they
were servile. They were in every way self-serving.

Yet, Jesus, in comparing the Pharisee to the tax collector
at prayer in the temple, says that it was the tax collector
rather than the Pharisee who went home justified. Dangerous stuff!

The point is that no amount of works can ever justify a
man: only faith and trust in a God who forgives. The Pharisee looks more like the religious man than the tax collector—and indeed, he is, if religion is primarily based upon
works and the Law. But, if true religion is based upon grace,

faith, and forgiveness, then that tax collector, as he acknowl-
edges his sins and his need of God's mercy, is "not very far
from the kingdom of heaven."

There is more here in this teaching of Jesus than it is possible to swallow at one time. Indeed, it is almost true to say
that in two thousand years, the church has never really taken
it all on board, in all its fullness. It is supremely the saints,
however, who vindicate the truth of this sublime teaching of
Jesus. Clearly, the saints do not claim any righteousness of
their own and are the first to "raise their eyes to heaven,"
knowing in every bone of their body their deep need of God
and his grace.

The Witness of the Saints

SAINT AELRED OF RIEVAULX (ca. 1109–67)

"When I was in deadly fear of everlasting damnation,
He comforted me and gave me life," wrote Aelred to his sister. "When I was cast down into the depths of despair, He
lifted me up again in perfect hope. And when I was most es-
tranged from Him, He came to me with His great benefits to
stir me to turn to Him again."

Often called the Bernard of the north, Aelred was the
son of a married Saxon priest from Hexham, and for some
years, young Aelred served with some distinction at the
court of King David of Scotland, the son of the saintly St.
Margaret of Scotland.

Aelred's father had secured the favor of the king of the
Scots, who frequently held his court only just across the hills
from Hexham at Roxburgh. From his earliest days, Aelred
formed close, lasting, and passionate friendships. At a young
age, he had formed such a friendship with Henry, King
David's son. "I lived with him from the cradle," says Aelred,
"we grew up together in boyhood; we knew each other in
adolescence." Furthermore, Aelred was much trusted by the
king and felt for his royal patron an admiration and affec-
tion which he never lost.

One day, while he was on the king's business at York in
1134, Aelred heard about the new Cistercian monastery at

Rievaulx. He decided at once to visit it. He immediately fell in love with the place, and after passing the customary three days in the hospice was received as a novice into that community. "When, in truth," Aelred writes later in life, "it pleased our good Lord to reprove the wanderer, to lift the fallen, and with his healing touch to cleanse the leper, abandoning all worldly hopes, I entered a monastery." In 1143, he became abbot of Revesby, and four years later returned to Rievaulx as abbot at the tender age of only thirty-eight. He remained abbot at Rievaulx for the next twenty years, and as such was in fact the head of the whole English Cistercian congregation.

During his time, the numbers of monks at Rievaulx rose dramatically, so that on great feast days, as Aelred's biographer is proud to tell us, "the church was packed with the brethren as to resemble a bee hive." So forgiving and loving was the abbot at all times, that we are told he never dismissed one monk in all his years as abbot.

His most important written works are his *Mirror Charity* (commissioned personally by none other than St. Bernard) and his book *Spiritual Friendship*, which is a kind of Christian answer to the classical book on *Friendship* by Cicero. "God is friendship," maintains Aelred, who himself enjoyed passionate and intimate relationships with his brethren, of which he is not ashamed to tell us in his writings.

He was canonized in 1191.

Our Experience

There can be little doubt that a post-Freudian age would classify Aelred as homosexual in his sexual orientation, as we like to say nowadays. On his own admission, he fell madly in love with his monks and novices, and although he clearly had many affairs of the heart, close and passionate relationships and friendships, he found direction, purpose, and, in the end, the redemption of his sexuality in God as he finally made the connection which was indeed the gospel for him, which can be summed up in the phrase, "God is friendship."

Aelred succeeded in avoiding two pitfalls. He refused to deny his nature by trying to suppress what he truly was. At the same time, he refused to become the slave to that nature by allowing it to rule his life, or by trying to rewrite his moral theology around his mistakes, his weaknesses, or even his feelings. Instead, he followed the way of grace, which is always a paradox. His vision of God as friendship meant that it was love (sexual and divine love) which led him *through* the pitfalls to express, and not repress, all that he was and would become in God and through God to his intimate friends and lovers. It is of the highest significance that the Hebrew language, unlike Greek, has only one word for love—*ahava*. Hence, the Judeo-Christian tradition should not divide love into different categories, but rather sees them all as belonging to each other. So for Aelred, God was in his friendships and his friendships belonged to God, who is himself love. That does not mean that Aelred got it right immediately. He fell into the ditch many times on his own admission, but what kept him from staying in the ditch and enabled him to move on was his continual reliance upon forgiveness, grace, and the infinite opportunity to make a new start. He did not need to settle for second best or to justify his actions—or, worse still, just try to make the best of a bad job, as we say.

The glorious thing about being a Christian is that we do not always have to be right, and that we have the freedom to fail—many times. Aelred kept his eyes continuously on the mystery of the Word made flesh—that great contradiction of Christianity which is such a stumbling block to those with a Greek mind and outlook. For in the end, after all the analysis, probing, and discussion (and there is plenty of that in Aelred's writings), he is still traveling toward that heavenly city, knowing that there are no easy answers on the way, that problems are indeed solutions in disguise, and that, in the end, perfect love casts out fear—that deadly weapon of the devil who would always try to seduce us into settling for the second best and justifying our actions in the process. The real enemy of the best and of holiness is the self-justifying virtue of the Pharisee; for the alternative to sin is not so much virtue as worship in which all our yearnings, desires, and drives find their ultimate expression, consummation, and fulfillment.

God is indeed friendship, but we must never allow friendship to become our God, otherwise it will become a demon with the terrifying capacity to destroy us.

WEEK THREE: FRIDAY

The scribes and the Pharisees brought a woman who had been caught in adultery, and placing her in the midst they said to him, "Teacher, this woman has been caught in the act of adultery. Now in the law Moses commanded us to stone such. What do you say about her?" This they said to test him, that they might have some charge to bring against him. Jesus bent down and wrote with his finger on the ground. And as they continued to ask him, he stood up and said to them, "Let him who is without sin among you be the first to throw a stone at her." And once more he bent down and wrote with his finger on the ground. But when they heard it, they went away, one by one, beginning with the eldest, and Jesus was left alone with the woman standing before him. Jesus looked up and said to her, "Woman, where are they? Has no one condemned you?" She said, "No one, Lord." And Jesus said, "Neither do I condemn you; go, and do not sin again." (John 8:3–11)

The Witness of Scripture

What did the Jewish Law say about adultery? The rabbi said, "Every Jew must die before he will commit idolatry, murder or adultery." Quite specifically, the book of Leviticus tells us that the sin of adultery carries the death penalty. "If a man commits adultery with the wife of his neighbor, both the adulterer and the adulteress shall be put to death" (Lev. 20:10) The Mishnah specifically dictates that death by stoning is the penalty for a girl who is betrothed and who then commits adultery.

The religious leaders were only repeating the law when they came to Jesus. What could he say? So, what does Jesus have to say about adultery? First, it is a sin ("Go and do not sin again"). Secondly, it is a sin which we should resolve either not to commit, or, if we have committed it, resolve not to commit again. In other words, adultery is not a good thing! Yet, at the same time, clearly it is not the worst sin or the ultimate sin deserving condemnation or the ultimate punishment (death by stoning).

What was Jesus doing, we might well ask, when he bent down to write in the sand? Was he playing for time? Was he just simply embarrassed by the whole hideous scene? One late Armenian manuscript suggests, "He himself, bowing his head, was writing with his finger on the earth to declare their sins, and they were seeing their several sins written on the stones in front of them"—the very stones that they would have to pick up and throw at the woman.

Whatever the explanation, we must not miss the most poignant and important point of all. "Let him who is without sin among you be the first to throw a stone at her." There was only one present who fell into that category—namely, Jesus himself. Little wonder that all the rest walk away and he alone is left with the woman. So, he who is without sin, has chosen for all humankind not to cast a stone or to condemn, but to forgive. We can say that of all sins and for all sinners.

The one who has done nothing wrong and who knows all is the only one who has the right to choose to forgive all and to condemn none. The law has not been violated, or abolished, but simply transformed from a law of condemnation to a new law of forgiveness and righteousness based upon the righteousness of God himself.

The Witness of the Saints

SAINT MARGARET OF CORTONA (1247–97)

Margaret was the daughter of a farmer of Laviano in Tuscany. When she was only seven years old, her mother died, and the woman whom her father subsequently married proved to be an unsympathetic and uncaring stepmother. Margaret was a spirited and pleasure-loving child, and she met, while still very young, an attractive cavalier from Montepulciano with whom she fell madly in love. One night, she eloped with him to his castle where she was to live openly with him, as his mistress, for the next nine years. She caused much scandal, especially, we are told, "when she rode through the streets of Montepulciano on a superb horse and splendidly attired." She bore her young, passionate lover, who never married her, one son.

One day, her young lover set off on horseback, accompanied by his dog, to visit his estates. He never returned. Margaret kept watch night and day for the return of her lover until, after several days, the dog returned alone. The dog plucked at Margaret's dress until she followed the faithful animal through the woods to the foot of an oak tree. There the dog scratched in the ground to uncover the mangled body of Margaret's lover, obviously murdered, thrown into the pit, and covered with leaves.

This tragedy proved to be the turning point in Margaret's life. After returning all her lover's possessions to his relatives, she set out with her little son for her father's home to ask for his acceptance and forgiveness. Her father refused to admit her to his home. Margaret was compelled to set out on the road, walking with her child. She walked to Cortona, where there was an order of Friars Minor, of whose gentleness with sinners she had often heard.

On arriving in Cortona, she and her son were taken in for a while by two ladies—Marinana and Raneria—who, on hearing her sad tale, subsequently introduced her to the local Franciscan community. For three years, Margaret struggled hard with fierce temptations to return to her old life or even to earn money by prostitution. However, the Franciscans helped her to find a stable, emotional, and spiritual life, while at the same time, Margaret began to earn her living by nursing and caring for the sick and the poor.

After about three years, she began to experience in the depths of her inner life the real love of Christ for her soul, through prayer, penance, and fasting. She became a member of the Third Order of St. Francis, wearing the simple habit and living in a small cottage where she was a recluse and contemplative. Her little boy was now growing up, and after some basic schooling at Arezzo, he entered the Franciscan Order.

Margaret, meanwhile, rapidly advanced in the life of the Spirit and the life of prayer, in which she experienced remarkable revelations from Christ. At first, Margaret had nursed people in her own cottage, but after a while she was joined by other women attracted to the life of ministry and prayer. The city council of Cortona was persuaded to assist Margaret and her nursing sisters in starting a hospital called Spedale di Santa Maria della Misericordia.

Her last years were spent in extreme austerity of life and in continuous prayer, during which God favored her with remarkable supernatural charismata. On the day of her death, at the age of fifty, she was publicly acclaimed as a saint, and the citizens of Cortona in the same year began to build a church in her honor, although she was not formally canonized until 1728.

She is generally depicted with the dog who led her to her lover's body and to the turning point in her life, where she found her heavenly Lover, Savior, Master, and Friend.

Our Experience

Margaret of Cortona takes her place in the procession and witness of the saints, as the woman taken in adultery takes her place in the gospel record. Wherever the gospel is preached, according to the words of Jesus, that story of that woman (from the various traditions) will always be told; for the tradition of Mary from Magdala, in whatever form we receive it, is, in the proverbial nutshell, the Good News.

It is sad, though perhaps understandable, that the church and indeed post-Christian society pays more attention to sexual sins than to almost any other sin, which is almost exactly the very opposite of the amount of attention that Jesus gives to this aspect of sin in the New Testament. Perhaps all this is because sexual sins wound our pride and demand that we stay very close to grace, forgiveness, and redemptive love. "How on earth could I have done a thing like that?" we are tempted to say. All sin wounds God, but it is pride, malice, hardness of heart, and contempt for his holy word that wound God most.

In the Old Testament, it was precisely hardness of heart which the Jew regarded as the terrible sin. For St. Thomas Aquinas, it was the sin of insensitivity, apathy, or indifference, which was most deadly. Such attitudes cut us off from reaching out to God for his healing and forgiving touch. For if we are insensitive and indifferent (that hardness of heart which was so deadly for the Jew), we shall probably avoid the temptations of the flesh and remain free from the sins of adultery and fornication, but at the same time, we shall probably be in serious danger of remaining indifferent also to God's love, which he longs to extend to us every day. The only trouble with being psychologically whole is that you might well end up by being irredeemable!

So we should not be too shocked to discover that it is the penitent prostitute, the alcoholic, and the drug user who, because they know most strongly their need of God, are the first into the kingdom of heaven.

However, we need to be neither sentimental nor judgmental about sexual sins, but rather just utterly realistic, knowing that in the realm of sexuality, if the ego is in the driver's seat, we are probably heading straight for disaster and the ditch. For in the area of our sexuality we are most widely open to self-delusion. Yet, in all of this we are truly called to love: to love people and to use things. The continuing temptation is to use people and to love things. If joy is the serious business of heaven, then it could well be that sex is intended to be fun on earth. However, it is not intended to be reduced to an entertainment. The sexual expression of love is intended for two people who take each other seriously enough to enjoy each other and who are totally committed to each other. We must always take people sufficiently seriously to respect their dignity, so that we would never seek to abuse them or to use them for our own selfish ends. Truth to tell, sexual sins are never the result of loving too much, but rather of not loving enough. True love demands not only the surrender of the body, but of everything that we are and all that we have, first to God, and through God to our neighbor.

WEEK THREE: SATURDAY

Then they cast him [Stephen] out of the city and stoned him; and the witnesses laid down their garments at the

feet of a young man named Saul. And as they were stoning Stephen, he prayed, "Lord Jesus, receive my spirit."
And he knelt down and cried with a loud voice, "Lord, do
not hold this sin against them." And when he had said
this, he fell asleep. (Acts 7:58–60)

The Witness of Scripture

The parallels between the record of Stephen's death and
the death of Christ are, to say the least, striking in the extreme. In both cases, false witnesses were produced, and in
both cases the charge was blasphemy. The first word on the
lips of Jesus on the cross was a prayer for his executioners,
and his last word was to commend his spirit into the hands
of his Father. Stephen utters the same prayers in essence, only
in reverse order.

And it was the last words of Stephen which clearly struck
home with Paul, who now enters the story which he eventually will dominate.

Luke, as a writer, historian, and artist, introduces Saul
with great subtlety. It was the forgiveness of the gospel which
was to be the piece of grit that eventually produced the
wound of saving knowledge in Paul's mind. The Law was
there to deal with forgiveness in Paul's book, and yet he
knew in his heart that it had not dealt with it at all for him.
Here was this remarkable young man, then, praying to this
Jesus and asking him to forgive his murderers. Could this be
what Paul and the Law had been seeking for so long and yet
never quite found?

On that tragic day, Paul stood on the edge of life, observing humanity at its worst and at its best, and all in a few
square yards and in a few moments of time. Yet, what came
so clearly through the anger and the murderous hatred was
a whole new way of life: unconditional forgiveness.

Paul almost certainly had not witnessed the death of
Jesus in Jerusalem. Yet, he had witnessed an almost identical
scene only weeks later in the stoning of Stephen. If this contradictory behavior were to catch on, it could turn the whole
world upside down. It must be stopped at all costs: the survival of law and order depends upon it.

And yet, could it be that this is what the world has been waiting for—that "greater love" which will unconditionally forgive? This could be not so much the end of the old way of life but, rather, the beginning of a totally new way of living.

The Witness of the Saints

SAINT THOMAS MORE (1478–1535)

At the age of fifty-seven, as Lord Chancellor of England, Thomas More had been tried and found guilty of treason on perjured evidence. The penalty for treason was to be hanged, drawn, and quartered. More's final words to the judges were:

"The blessed apostle St. Paul, as we read in the Acts of the Apostles, was present and consented to the death of St. Stephen, and kept their clothes that stoned him to death and yet be they now both twain Holy Saints in Heaven, and shall continue there friends for ever. So I verily trust and shall therefore rightly pray, that though your lordships have now here in earth been judges to my condemnation, we may yet hereafter in Heaven merrily all meet together to our everlasting salvation."

A man of brilliance, humor, letters, and learning, Thomas More was also a statesman and a deeply committed Christian. The author of the Latin classics *Utopia and The Dialogue of Comfort* written in his prison cell, More had been appointed, at the age of fifty-one, Lord Chancellor of England under King Henry VIII. Much loved by his family and friends, including that supreme humanist, Erasmus, he was famous in his day for his learning and his proverbial wit, but above all for his life of faith and virtue.

He died because he refused to be false to his conscience, which he knew needed to be always informed and not merely led by the whim of passion and feeling. Although he lived at a time when popes were infamous for their immorality and laxity, he nevertheless believed in the supremacy of the papal office over kings and princes, and in the end, it was the papal supremacy (as opposed to the royal supremacy) for which he died.

In early life, he tested his vocation to be a monk and led an ascetic life of prayer and fasting. However, he decided that his call was not to leave the world, but rather to seek to influence it for good and for the gospel. So he rose to the highest honor that any layman could attain in the realm of England, next to the king. When King Henry declared that his earlier marriage had been null and void in spite of the Pope's refusal to declare it so, Parliament passed the Act of Succession, and More, along with all the other leaders of the nation, was compelled to take the oath of allegiance to King Henry as prescribed in that act. He felt that he could not do so "without the jeopardy of" his soul.

So it was that he was tried and found guilty of treason. The king intervened and insisted that More, as a peer of the realm, should not be hanged, drawn, and quartered, but that he should be beheaded.

"No more than parliament could make a law that God were not God, could parliament make the king supreme head of the church," was More's insistence to the end. "We are not bound to admire the whole of More's life," writes Lord Longford, "although it has attracted many....The church recognizes that a flawed life can be rendered sublime by its final moments or...its later stages." There can be little doubt that in the end, Thomas More received that same generous forgiveness which he himself so graciously and generously gave to his persecutors.

Our Experience

There is no doubt that the church is most like Jesus when it is ready to forgive most, and least like Jesus when it puts premature judgment before forgiveness.

Nearly all the last words of the Christian martyrs, like the last words of Jesus himself on the cross, have offered forgiveness to their persecutors. As such, all the last words of Christian martyrs in many different languages and throughout the ages are an echo of the first words of Jesus concerning his murderers on Calvary: "Father, forgive...."

John's Gospel, reflects upon the measure of Christ's love shown in the upper room on the night before his passion.

"Having loved his own, he loved them to the end—the ut-termost." Forgiveness is the only road which can go all the way with love. That is why marriage is a sacrament: it is a sign of God's limitless love. Wherever we draw a line, God draws another line right through it. It is the sign of the cross, the sign of infinite love and therefore of infinite forgiveness. That is covenant love, and as such it is unreasonable! The reasonable sort of love for which we are tempted to settle is more of a contract than a covenant. You keep your side of the bargain and I will keep mine. So a contract draws up certain kinds of cautious guidelines, while a covenant allows for no such provisions. A covenant is totally binding, yet it is in its bondage that we alone can find freedom—the free-dom to fail.

Think what kind of freedom there is in a covenant of love. I do not have to be a wild success. I can afford to fail. I do not have to be a good husband or a good wife, any more than the prodigal son was a good son. He was a bad son for a long time, but he was a son, and there was no way that he could settle for just becoming a more or less reasonably good servant. Surely the burden of a trial marriage (or a trial sonship) would be intolerable. Every morning I would have to undergo a kind of assessment on how I was doing to see whether we could go on with the arrangement!

I shall probably need to be a bad husband or a bad wife before I can have a good marriage! But in the meantime, and indeed, until the end of time, I can draw on the credit of God's forgiveness, being ready to offer that forgiveness and ready to receive it. Forgiveness is the cement between the building blocks of love.

But of course, none of this is reasonable to expect, any more than it was reasonable to expect Stephen or Thomas More to forgive their murderers. Love (and therefore forgive-ness) has to go a long way ahead of reason. In fact, infinite love and infinite forgiveness are always the joker in the pack, but only for those who are willing to go all the way, even to death.

Yet notice how *THE* breakthrough was established in the new order of love by Jesus *SOMEWHERE*, once upon a time. He was the first through the hoop. All the others are but copies and echoes of that first, most revolutionary contradiction in the history of the world. Now, by the grace of Calvary, *EVERYWHERE* and at all times and in all places, many throughout history have vindicated the power of unconditional forgiveness which always triumphs over all the terrible atrocities of which humanity is capable, even to the point of murder and death.

For in a sense that is the point of it all. The last enemy, after all, is death. We are called to love our enemies, even to the end and even unto death, and to defeat the enemy in the process.

Healing and Renewal

And he touched my mouth and said: "Behold, this has touched your lips; your guilt is taken away, and your sin forgiven."

INTRODUCING WEEK FOUR

Healing, renewal, and life all belong together. We cannot receive any of these gifts apart from the Giver, whom we should desire above and beyond any or all of his gifts.

Nine times out of ten, we are only cured and not healed. It is significant that although ten lepers were cured of leprosy, only one of them was also healed. He was an outsider (a Samaritan); he was converted (he turned around, we are told); and he came back to the feet of Jesus whom he worshiped as Lord, giving thanks. In many ways, that is the classical formula for renewal, healing, and resurrection.

Although in our baptism we are born again of water and the Spirit, all of us, at various points on the journey of faith, begin to stand still in our faith—like those two disciples on the road to Emmaus. They stood still, we are told, "looking sad." Whenever Christians stop traveling, growing, and changing, they stand still, and it will not be long before they begin to look sad. Joy goes out of faith and we begin to become soured, ungrateful, tired Christians. This is a recurring pattern, not only for individual disciples at various points in their lives, but also in the history of the church over the centuries.

We all need, personally and corporately, that "second touch"—that "further touch" of Christ's new life to convince us of forgiveness, to heal the diseases of our souls, and to raise us up to that new life which is the gift of God to his people.

We need, therefore, a continuing confirmation in the life of the Holy Spirit, of which the Sacrament of Confirmation is the particular sign in our church. That daily increase in his Holy Spirit for which the bishop prays at Confirmation is what healing and renewal are all about. So often we want the gifts of the Holy Spirit without the Giver.

The saints, therefore, are not peculiar. They are what all Christians should be. At every stage of their journey of faith, they knew their need of God, and they were not ashamed to be brought to their knees in order that they might ask for it. "O come to my heart, Lord Jesus, make room in my heart for thee."

Yet, Christian discipleship is a lifelong journey, and renewal is for all God's people, all the time, not just for people who like that kind of thing from time to time. Furthermore, renewal is something we receive rather than achieve. We need to avail ourselves of the ministry of healing, through the laying-on of hands, or with the anointing of holy oil. We need to use retreats and special weekends away in groups to receive that "second touch." We need from time to time to confess our sins, and to receive the gospel reassurance of God's love and forgiveness. We need to ask God for all the necessary gifts of his Holy Spirit for the work of mission and ministry in his church.

So, renewal is not doing some new thing, but rather doing the same old, well-tried things in a new spirit. It is essentially a question of drawing ever more closely to Jesus in the likeness of his death and resurrection, so that we also can be raised from the death of sin to newness of life in the power of the Holy Spirit.

There should be nothing divisive about renewal in the Spirit, nothing that smacks of envy. All the gifts are given for the sake of the whole Body, and no one gift is essential to all, except the gift of love. So, we need to pray again in our day for the renewal of God's people in faith, hope, love and holiness, always insisting that renewal will begin with me, *now*, today. For, in the words of the psalmist, "Today, if you will hear his voice," you shall know his power (Ps. 95:7).

Questions for Personal Reflection or Discussion in Groups

1. What is the difference between being cured and being healed, and in what ways will the differences show?

2. Christian formation and spiritual direction are essential ingredients in the whole process of renewal. What are the distinctive characteristics of the ministry of spiritual direction, and in what ways should we be encouraging the development of this ministry in the church today?

3. Read again chapter 12 of the first epistle to the Corinthians. What lessons can we learn from that chapter for our church today in terms of ministry and the gifts of the Holy Spirit?

4. If healing is an essential and central ingredient in the gospel message, why are we so afraid of it, and what should we be doing to make sure that such a ministry is more available in the life of the church?

WEEK FOUR: MONDAY

So Naaman came with his horses and chariots, and halted at the door of Elisha's house. And Elisha sent a messenger to him, saying, "Go and wash in the Jordan seven times, and your flesh shall be restored, and you shall be clean." But Naaman was angry, and went away, saying, "Behold, I thought that he would surely come out to me, and stand, and call on the name of the Lord his God, and wave his hand over the place, and cure the leper. Are not Abana and Pharphar, the rivers of Damascus, better than all the waters of Israel? Could I not wash in them, and be clean?" So he turned and went away in a rage. But his servants came near to him and said, "My father, if the prophet had commanded you to do some great thing, would you not have done it? How much rather, then, when he says to you, 'Wash, and be clean?'" So he went down and dipped himself seven times in the Jordan, according to the word of the man of God; and his flesh was restored like the flesh of a little child, and he was clean. (2 Kings 5:9–14)

The Witness of Scripture

In the eyes of the world, Naaman was a successful man in every way. His very name in Arabic means "charming, pleasant." Yet, it is such worldly people who find it so difficult to come to terms with the ways of God and, particularly, with their own weaknesses. He held a high position as commander-in-chief in the army of the king of Syria, yet the one blight on his life was a skin disease of some kind. The word used here refers to a general skin disability rather than specifically to leprosy.

He had probably told himself many times that, if only he could be rid of this affliction, his life would be perfect and complete. Yet, as our story shows, Naaman had far more serious disorders in his life than this skin disease. He needed to learn his real needs and to accept his weakness and frailty as a human being. Like so many who appear rich and successful, underneath he was wretched, poor, and something of a disaster.

So he does not really come to the prophet to be healed, but rather (in the Hebrew) "to be rid" of this affliction. He supposes that Elisha will make a great fuss of him, as everyone usually did. However, this was not the case. Elisha does not even come to meet or greet him. He just sends a messenger with a somewhat off-handed message, instructing Naaman to go and wash himself seven times in the muddy River Jordan.

Naaman is offended—he is not used to this kind of treatment. Only the concern of his servants finally persuades him to do as Elisha has told him to do. For the truth is that Elisha has diagnosed the real disease of Naaman's soul: pride and contempt for God's holy word.

Naaman was successful in being rid of his skin complaint, but he also learned a real spiritual lesson from this encounter. What he wanted and what he needed were two different things. Nevertheless, God in the end was able to give Naaman both his wants and his needs, and to heal his soul as well as the ailments of his body. True renewal involves a total diagnosis and a total healing.

The Witness of the Saints

SAINT FRANCIS DE SALES (1567–1622)

St. Francis de Sales, born in the Savoy country in 1567, was the bishop evangelist of the Counter-Reformation. From his early youth he had never been physically strong, and only after much opposition from his father to his religious vocation was he finally ordained to the priesthood in 1593.

He was called at the outset of his ministry to work in the area of Geneva, the metropolis and mecca of the Reformation in general and of Calvinism in particular. In those days, to proclaim Catholicism in that city was no mean undertaking. It almost cost Francis his life on several occasions.

It was not long before Francis began to write and to issue tracts as well as to preach sermons aimed at recalling people to the faith of the Catholic church. After being bishop coadjutor, he succeeded to the See of Geneva in 1602 and took up his residence in Annecy, with a household organized on lines of the strictest economy. He devised an educational program for teaching the Christian faith throughout the whole of his diocese and gave a prominent place in his ministry to spiritual formation and direction. One of the people who came to him for such spiritual counseling and friendship was St. Jane Frances de Chantal, who was eventually to found the Order of the Visitation in 1610. So it was that the two saints became lifelong friends.

The Introduction to the Devout Life, Francis' most famous book and one which has influenced many Christians over the ages, grew out of casual notes and jottings of instruction originally written for Mme. de Chamoisy, a cousin to Francis by marriage who had placed herself under his spiritual direction.

The whole story of Francis' life is immensely edifying, and it was as much the sheer beauty of holiness of his life as his teaching, preaching, and writing which influenced so strongly the Counter-Reformation and the church of his day. He died in intense pain at the hands of primitive and crude physicians at the age of fifty-six, and the last word that he was heard to utter at his death was quite simply the word

"Jesus." In naming him the patron saint of journalists in 1923, Pope Pius XI commended St. Francis de Sales as "the spiritual writer perhaps the most suited of all to meet the religious needs of the world at the present day." There is much to suggest that such a commendation is still true today.

Our Experience

In the confirmation service of the old Anglican Book of Common Prayer, as the bishop laid his hands upon the head of the confirmation candidate, he prayed that this renewed Christian would "daily increase" in God's Holy Spirit until he or she finally attained to God's heavenly kingdom.

Renewal is not preceded by some dramatic flash of insight. Naaman wanted the prophet to come out of his house and give him a fix of healing. Instead, he was told to go and wash patiently seven times in the local river, just like people did every day of their lives. Renewal is a gradual process. It is not something you get once and for all and can then place on record on your resumé as a one-time achievement! In the Lord's Prayer we are taught to pray for *daily* bread. That is because yesterday's manna is no earthly use today. That bread of the kingdom, like renewal in the Holy Spirit, is a gift from God that needs to be received again and again with eucharist and thanksgiving.

Of course, in one sense, you cannot add anything to baptism. It is a once-for-all, all-sufficient gift. Yet, in another sense, we need to draw upon our baptismal treasure each and every day. The Christian is a pilgrim and needs daily food for the journey. The Scriptures, the sacraments, and prayer are great reserves of food for the hungry soul. Just as physically we need a balanced diet, so, too, do we need a balanced spiritual diet. Renewal for Anglican Christians is perhaps best summarized in seven steps: daily commitment to Scripture, sacraments, and life in the Spirit; issuing in study, stewardship, service, and sacrifice.

In all of this we need the assistance and support of a spiritual director or soul friend, as we prefer to call such a ministry in the Anglican tradition. It is in the Celtic tradition that we meet the figure of the "soul friend." The Irish word *anmchara* is rendered as "spiritual guide" or "spiritual director." Of course, it should go without saying that the real spiritual director is the Holy Spirit. Yet, it is the particular delight of the Holy Spirit to form the Body of Christ, and as we know from the teaching of Jesus, the quorum for that body is only two or three, unlike the quorum for a synagogue which was ten. The spiritual director and the Christian disciple, guided by the Holy Spirit, constitute the church, and it is in the context of the church that we receive the blessing and guidance of the Holy Spirit. An individual hot line to God is less than a Christian concept.

For example, it is significant that Jesus sent out his disciples two by two. As Peter Wagner reminds us so forcefully, "There are no lone rangers in the kingdom." So St. Augustine of Hippo reminds us that "no one can walk without a guide." St. Basil from the Eastern tradition warns us that "to believe that one does not need counsel is great pride." We do well to remember that where two or three are together on the road to resurrection, Jesus makes himself present and available, as surely as he did to those two disciples on the road to Emmaus, and always for counsel, encouragement, and to give a new direction to their path.

Spiritual direction was a particular ministry of Francis de Sales, who in his writings outlines the work and ministry of spiritual direction such as he gave to Mme. de Chamoisy. "And why should we wait to be masters of ourselves in that which concerns the spirit," wrote St. Francis, "since we are not so in what concerns the body? Do we not know that doctors, when they are sick, call other doctors to judge on the remedies that are right for them?" (sermon on the feast of Our Lady of Sorrows).

The ministry of St. Francis de Sales was essentially a renewal ministry. The great motto with which both Mme de Chamoisy and the bishop headed their letters was always *Vive Jesus:* "Live Jesus." Each and every letter ends with "God be praised." For Francis and for the Salesian Order, as for St. Paul, to be alive was to "live Jesus" and to help Christ to be formed in others by the work of the Holy Spirit. As St. Paul said it so forcefully, "I no longer live, but Christ lives in me" (Gal. 2:20.) That is commitment to a lifetime of renewal.

WEEK FOUR: TUESDAY

And they came bringing to him a paralytic carried by four men. And when they could not get near him because of the crowd, they removed the roof above him; and when they had made an opening, they let down the pallet on which the paralytic lay. And when Jesus saw their faith, he said to the paralytic, "My son, your sins are forgiven." Now some of the scribes were sitting there, questioning in their hearts, "Why does this man speak thus? It is blasphemy! Who can forgive sins but God alone?" And immediately Jesus, perceiving in his spirit that they thus questioned within themselves, said to them, "Why do you question thus in your hearts? Which is easier, to say to the paralytic, 'Your sins are forgiven,' or to say, 'Rise, take up your pallet and walk?' But that you may know that the Son of man has authority on earth to forgive sins" - he said to the paralytic - "I say to you, rise, take up your pallet and go home." And he rose, and immediately took up the pallet and went out before them all; so that they were all amazed and glorified God, saying, "We never saw anything like this!" (Mark 2:3–12)

The Witness of Scripture

Right at the outset of Mark's Gospel, Jesus puts together forgiveness, healing, and renewal as a package deal and sets it within the community of faith—namely, the church. We are told that Jesus was at home, preaching the word of God, and that the people were gathered together around him. Such is the true nature of the church. The church is the place of the real presence of Jesus, where the word is preached and where two or three (at least) are gathered together in his name. It is in this context that forgiveness, healing, and renewal are possible.

Four friends of the paralyzed man are determined against all odds to get their friend to Jesus. Such was their faith and such was the crowd, that the only way to Jesus was, literally, through the roof.

Notice that when Jesus sees the faith of the four friends, he heals the paralytic. The church is the community of faith in which each lives and prays for the others. Whenever we go to church, into the presence of Jesus, we need to take someone else with us in our hearts and in our prayers.

Then Jesus deliberately puts together forgiveness, healing, and renewal of life—and he is the Lord and minister of all three of these. Yet, the activity of forgiveness, healing, and renewal constitute a family business—the business of the church—which is intended to be an environment in which all three are continuously at work for those who are near and for those who are far off: for those inside and those outside the church.

The genius of the Benedictine movement was its ability to reconstitute the wider medieval church around communities and cells of healing and renewal of life. Sadly, the Benedictine movement became an end in itself and not simply a means to an end, and itself soon became desperately in need of healing and renewal. Such is often the history of renewal movements in the life of the church.

The Witness of the Saints

SAINT BENEDICT (ca. 480–ca. 550)

In 1964, as the European Community increasingly emerged as a real possibility for the twenty-first century, Pope Paul VI proclaimed St. Benedict to be the patron saint of Europe.

Almost certainly not a priest, but a layman, Benedict established his Rule for the conduct of community life. This was to become one of the foundation documents upon which the European culture and, indeed, the whole of Western culture was built. Courtesy, hospitality, and the pursuit of work, prayer, and study formed the basic principles on which a free society could grow and flourish.

Born in the district of Nursia, in Umbria, central Italy, Benedict was sent to Rome at an early age to pursue a "liberal education." He found the life at Rome full of vice, corruption, and licentiousness, and so he escaped without telling anyone of his plans. He made his way to the mountainous area some thirty miles or so outside Rome. However, he soon discovered that absence from the temptations of metropolitan life in Rome was not, in itself, enough: God was calling him to step out in faith as a solitary and to abandon the world.

In search of that solitude, Benedict set out again and climbed farther into the hills of Subiaco. In this deserted place in the wild and rocky countryside, the young Benedict found a monk called Romanus who assisted him, clothing him and bringing to him for the next three years the simplest of daily fare that Benedict drew up in a basket.

Gradually, other monks came to seek out the hermit Benedict. Benedict organized these stray monks into twelve monasteries, each with its own abbot. But again in 525, he withdrew with a few monks from Subiaco to the territory of Monte Cassino, which is a solitary elevation on the boundaries of the Campania, south of Rome on the way to Naples. Here he built two little chapels and then, eventually, the great building which was destined to become the most famous abbey in the Western world.

It was probably at this time that he drew up his famous Rule, which was to become such an important document for medieval society and culture. Legend tells us that he "cured the sick, relieved the distressed, distributed alms and food to the poor," and is said to have raised the dead on more than one occasion. It would seem that he did not intend to found an order for clerics, but rather for laymen. The domination of the order by priests is a later development. Benedict died in his chapel, standing in prayer with hands uplifted, and was buried at Monte Cassino in the same grave as his sister, St. Scholastica. French tradition maintains that the remains of St. Benedict were translated to Fleury in 703. This is contested by the monks of Monte Cassino, where excavations made possible by the wanton destruction of the abbey in the Second World War yielded substantial remains, regarded by many as those of St. Benedict and St. Scholastica.

Our Experience

For a healthy, physical life we need rhythm and regularity. There is something unhealthy and even destructive about erratic behavior that lurches from one enthusiasm and obsession to another. Stability provides the environment for growth and development.

It is not accidental, therefore, that stability was the "fourth vow" of the Benedictines in the Rule of St. Benedict. It gives to spirituality the necessary, matter-of-fact, everyday rooted-ness which makes "bodily growth" possible and builds up the common life (Eph. 4:16). We see something of it in the injunction of Jesus to his first missionaries not to "go from house to house." So the Benedictine life is built upon proper stability and upon hospitality for the stranger or the visitor. In the Dark Ages, when family life and community life were breaking down, the Benedictine monasteries became cells of stable community with the abbot acting very much in the place of a father to his family. The daily life was built upon a rhythm of manual and mental work, prayer, and proper rest, work, feast and fast, winter, spring, summer, autumn, hours of sleep and all in a measure of the hours of a day, conse-crated by regular corporate worship.

The Rule of St. Benedict was simply a practical develop-ment of gospel life—life in the kingdom. The word "rule" is not a particularly helpful translation of the Latin *regula,* since it tends to suggest something rather legalistic or formalistic. Regularity and rhythm in life is more the image intended. Many Christians today who live in an age of fragmentation and the breakdown of family and community life have found great help by adapting Benedictine spirituality for their rule of life. Indeed, the spirituality of the Anglican Prayer Book is essentially Benedictine in flavor with its emphasis upon the daily office. The Rule must not degenerate into formal-ism, become an end in itself, or become a substitute for life in the spontaneity of the Holy Spirit. On the contrary, it is the structure which enables true spontaneity, and it is the Rule which can free us from the wrong kind of self-consciousness about our spiritual life and our spiritual temperature.

It is difficult to exaggerate the part played by the spiritu-ality, witness, and Rule of St. Benedict in the formation of European culture as the West moved through the Dark Ages into the flowering of the Middle Ages. The Benedictine mona-steries were truly citadels of light, human dignity, hospitality,

learning, courtesy, and care for the stranger, the poor, and
the homeless in a dark, divided, and warring world.

As the church is renewed in our day, Christians will increasingly live the Christian life in the context of communities of faith, in which the aged will be respected, the unborn
will be welcome, and hospitality will be the hallmark of Christian charity towards the stranger, the unwanted, the marginal-
ized, the homeless, and those who have no helper. But this
is essentially the work and witness of the whole Body corporately, in which individual members find their freedom
and all the necessary resources of the Spirit to live out the life
of the gospel message.

WEEK FOUR: WEDNESDAY

And they came to Bethsaida. And some people brought to
him a blind man, and begged him to touch him. And he
took the blind man by the hand, and led him out of the
village; and when he had spit on his eyes and laid his
hands upon him, he asked him, "Do you see anything?"
And he looked up and said, "I see men; but they look like
trees, walking." Then again he laid his hands upon his
eyes; and he looked intently and was restored, and saw
everything clearly. And he sent him away to his home,
saying, "Do not even enter the village." (Mark 8:22–26)

The Witness of Scripture

Healing and renewal are never a once-for-all experience.
It is a gradual process of illumination, enlightenment, and
growth in the Spirit.

It is important to see this miracle of the healing of the
blind man in the context in which Mark sets it. Jesus and his
disciples have just come from the second miraculous feed-
ing of the multitudes. The first time, you remember, Jesus
fed five thousand, and then, at the second miraculous feed-
ing, he apparently fed four thousand. The disciples and Jesus
had then immediately gotten into a boat and gone to the district of Dalmanutha. On the way, the disciples grew anxious,

because they had forgotten to bring any food with them. Jesus is almost driven to desperation by their blindness. ("Why do you discuss the fact that you have no bread? Do you not perceive, or understand....Having eyes, do you not see?") On two occasions, Jesus has provided all that they and the huge crowds could possibly have needed and more, and yet still the disciples are anxious, blind, and lacking in faith and perception.

Then they come immediately to Bethsaida. A blind beggar comes up to Jesus—a regular occurrence, it would seem from the gospel accounts. Yet, this time, Jesus ministers to the man with a "second touch." Unless we, too, are blind, surely we can see what Jesus is trying to tell his disciples as well as what he is trying to tell us.

We all need to grow daily in perception. Jesus is the patient teacher who is willing to minister to us and who sees the need for gradual healing, renewal, and growth in perception and insight. The good teacher knows that we do not take it all in the first time. So Jesus did not just feed the crowd once, but at least twice, and the chances are, I suspect, many times. He is prepared to stay with us in our blindness and to touch our lives for healing and renewal, not only a second time, but many times. We shall need not only that "second touch," but many other occasions, places, and ways in which we can feel his healing touch opening our eyes, ears, and hearts ever more widely, until we fully perceive the height, depth, length, and breadth of his great love.

The Witness of the Saints

GEORGE HERBERT (1593–1633)

"Thus he lived and thus he died like a saint, unspotted of the world, full of alms' deeds, full of humility and all the examples of a virtuous life." So his rather eulogistic biographer Isaac Walton summarizes the life of George Herbert, the seventeenth-century Anglican priest, poet, and essayist.

George Herbert was born the seventh of ten children on April 3, 1593, in Montgomeryshire on the border between England and Wales. On the death of his father, the Herbert family moved first to Oxford and then to London, where they lived at Charing Cross. George Herbert became a student at the famous Westminster School, just at the time when that other saintly Anglican figure, Lancelot Andrewes, was ending his tenure as Dean of Westminster Abbey. Elected a scholar of Westminster in 1605, he proceeded to Trinity College, Cambridge, as King's Scholar for a distinguished and scholarly career. Subsequently he was chosen as a Major Fellow of Trinity College and in 1620 was elected Public Orator of Cambridge University. His time as Public Orator brought him renown and praise from King James I, and his extensive correspondence at this time included such notable persons as Sir Francis Bacon and the now Bishop Lancelot Andrewes. Herbert's increasing renown at court would seem to have indicated a public career and the attainment of high office in church or state.

So it was that he delayed his ordination to the priesthood and chose rather to serve in Parliament as a representative for Montgomeryshire. After his ordination to the diaconate by the bishop of Lincoln on December 6, 1624, he was installed as a canon of Lincoln Cathedral and given the titular living of Leighton Bromswold. He was not actually ordained to the priesthood until 1630, after he had married a girl of noble family, Jane Danvers. All this time, Herbert could be forgiven for supposing that public service to an earthly king (such as James, of whom he thought so very highly) could be easily combined with service to a heavenly king.

The death of James I and the increasing influence of Nicholas Ferrar of the Little Gidding Community led Herbert to rethink all his priorities. He committed himself to reading the daily offices of the Prayer Book of the Church of England—both morning and evening. As a matter of interest, canons of Lincoln Cathedral to this day are required to recite an allotted psalm or psalms each day, so that the whole chapter recites the whole psalter daily. Herbert's particular responsibility was to recite daily Psalms 31 and 32. It was through his association with John Williams, Bishop of Lincoln, who was also Visitor to the Little Gidding Community, that Herbert's friendship with Nicholas Ferrar was cemented and strengthened.

All this amounted in the end to Herbert turning his back on London, London society, and parliamentary and court life, in order to become a country parish priest in the living of Fugglestone with Bemerton near Salisbury, where he spent the rest of his days with his family, dying at the early age of forty.

Herbert wrote sacred poetry and a famous prose work, *The Country Parson*, which embodies the ideal of Anglican spirituality and pastoral ministry. Many of his poems are used as hymns to this day: for example, "Teach me, my God and King," and "Let all the world in every corner sing."

Although he ended his days as an obscure country parson and lived only a short life, his name, his writings, and his influence have lived on in quite wonderful ways in the Anglican tradition.

Our Experience

Renewal is an ongoing process and experience whereby, in the words of Wesley, we are "changed from glory into glory." The saints are always most aware of their failings and shortcomings. "There is no proof of the presence of the Spirit which is more certain than a desire for ever greater grace," said St. Bernard (second sermon on St. Andrew).

The blind man at Bethsaida underwent a gradual process of healing before he could really see straight! Perhaps the most dangerous thing about the renewal movement in the church in recent years is its tendency to tempt people into believing that just because they have received one or more of the spectacular gifts of the Spirit (tears, tongues, healing) they have "arrived."

> Ah, but a man's reach should exceed his grasp,
> Or what's a heaven for?
>
> (Robert Browning)

We must never cease to press forward on our pilgrimage of faith, letting our desire for God always outstrip our apprehension of him. So yesterday's point of arrival must become today's point of departure, otherwise we shall simply get stuck. After all, the only difference between a rut and a grave is that a grave is just a little deeper than a rut.

"That which is good, sanctifying and spiritual for my brother below or beside me on the mountain side can be material, misleading, or bad for me. What I rightly allowed myself yesterday, I must perhaps deny myself today," wrote Teilhard de Chardin. G.K. Chesterton draws a helpful picture of the Christian pilgrim when he tells us that at one moment "the road points to the pub" on that journey of faith and growth in the spiritual life, but it will not be long before the "pub points back to the road" as life goes on.

Jesus promised us many "resting places" (not "mansions") in his Father's house. Those "resting places" were caravan sites where you could rest for the night in order to find strength and refreshment for tomorrow's journey.

Certainly the life of George Herbert was a pilgrimage during which what he allowed himself at one staging post of the journey, he was ready to deny himself farther down the road. We watch him moving through a career of great distinction, yet eventually outgrowing the need for worldly glory and human acclamation. He eventually found his fulfillment here on earth in the ministry of a "Country Parson," and as such he delighted to pasture and tend the Lord's sheep. He found in the pastoral ministry of a country parish all the ingredients necessary to encourage holiness of life and growth, detaching himself—to use his own words—from "the gilded baits of worldly love," preaching, teaching, and tending the souls committed to his care. He grew and taught his parishioners how to grow in renewal and holiness of life through regular prayer and the rhythm of fasting and feasting. Yet he died young—perhaps because he was still "traveling." His country parish never became a dead end. Rather, it was just another resting place on the great journey.

So renewal, healing, and refreshment are not ends in themselves. They are means to an end, and in the meantime we always need to recognize a right restlessness which refuses to settle for anything less than the vision of God. For that is our true end. Augustine was right: "We were made by God and for God, and our hearts are restless until they rest in God."

WEEK FOUR: THURSDAY

Upon my bed by night
I sought him whom my soul loves;
    I sought him, but found him not;
I called him, but he gave no answer.
    "I will rise now and go about the city,
In the streets and in the squares;
    I will seek him whom my soul loves."
I sought him, but found him not.
    The watchmen found me,
As they went about in the city.
    "Have you seen him whom my soul loves?"
Scarcely had I passed them,
    When I found him whom my soul loves.
I held him, and would not let him go
    until I had brought him into my mother's house,
    and into the chamber of her that conceived me....

Set me as a seal upon your heart,
As a seal upon your arm;
    for love is strong as death,
jealousy as cruel as the grave.
    Its flashes are flashes of fire,
a most vehement flame.
    Many waters cannot quench love,
neither can floods drown it.
    If a man offered for love
all the wealth of his house,
    it would be utterly scorned.
        (Song of Solomon 3:1–4; 8:6–7)

The Witness of Scripture

It is remarkable that the Song of Solomon, or the Song of Songs, is in the canon of the Old Testament. It is an outstanding work of love poetry. A song of great beauty and power, it has remarkable imagery, ranging from images of the field and garden to images of animal life and plant life.

Its dating, authorship, and origin are all problematical, yet such questions need not in any way detract from the usefulness of this great love poem for Christian devotion or indeed, from its powers of inspiration.

St. Bernard and the early Cistercians turned to it and used it frequently in their preaching and in their teaching. Many preachers use this book as an allegory of what they like to call "spiritual love," and even to apply it to our personal relationship with God in Christ. Yet, many of the commentaries speak of this as a "danger," possibly leading to "an erotic view of" our relationship with Christ.

To assume this is to miss the point and the purpose of including this book in the scriptural canon. To the Hebrew mind, there were no such categories of love as there were for the Greek mind. There is only one word in Hebrew for love, not three. Therefore, for the Jew, love was all of a piece. He was commanded to love God with all his love—"body, mind, and passions." So it is entirely proper to use the Song of Songs as a prayer of loving devotion to the God of Love who has shown that one, undivided love to us in the person of Jesus Christ—the bridegroom wedded to his church, the bride.

This kind of mystical theology was the inspiration of St. Bernard, Dante, St. John of the Cross, and St. Teresa of Avila in particular, though to a greater or lesser extent it has necessarily been an open secret among all the saints and among all God's holy people. There is no other way.

The Witness of the Saints

SAINT BERNARD (1090–1153)

Only those who are willing to reject worldly power at first are, in the end, most able to influence the world and to exercise true power over it to change it, and so to redirect the course of human history.

The life of St. Bernard of Clairvaux exhibits this paradox in every chapter. Bernard, the third son of a Burgundian noble, was sent by his father to Chatillon on the Seine, to pursue a complete course of studies in a college of secular canons.

From the outset, Bernard had all the advantages, talents, and prestigious gifts this world could offer, but at the early age of twenty-two, he counted everything "as so much garbage for the sake of the knowledge of Jesus Christ." He turned his back on all that this world had to offer and chose to go to Citeaux, where only a few years before, St. Stephen Harding had established the first monastery of that very strict interpretation of the Benedictine Rule, later to be known as Cistercian. Having first turned his back on the world and on his age, Bernard "was perhaps the greatest organizer of the Middle Ages." For Benedictinism had grown affluent, tired, and worldly, and was proving to be less effective for change and for the redirection of the church and the world of the twelfth century. So Bernard "dominated all other voices in his own century and changed more patterns of thought and sentiment than anyone else....Knowledge of God comes only through devotion to God in poverty, in simplicity and in solitude. Within his own generation, the Cistercian movement based on these principles was the greatest success story of the Middle Ages."

"To be poor with Christ" was his one concern. Bernard admits, "I chose Citeaux in preference to Cluny [the great, wealthy Benedictine monastery] not because I was not aware that the life there was excellent and lawful, but because... I was conscious my weak character needed a strong medicine."

So, based at Clairvaux as abbot from 1127 until his death, Bernard was called upon to give counsel on a whole range of temporal affairs across the whole of Christendom. He interceded in broken relations between kings and princes; he was strategic in helping to patch up the major papal schism of his day and in 1143, Eugene III, one of Bernard's spiritual "sons," was elected Pope. At Vezelay, Bernard preached the Second Crusade and motivated everyone from peasantry to aristocracy to march to the Holy Land to recover the holy places for Christ. Yet, he wrote with terrifying insight, "My burdened conscience and my life resemble some kind of fabled monster...a chimera of the century, acting neither as a monk nor as a layman...driven about through the abysses of the world."

At the age of sixty-three, on August 20, 1153, God took Bernard to himself. He had been abbot for thirty-eight years, and no less than sixty-eight monasteries had been founded from Clairvaux. Canonized in 1174 and known as the "mellifluous doctor," he was to influence the thought and spirituality of the centuries following his life. Dante meets Bernard in his *Divine Comedy* in the tenth sphere of the heavenly mysteries:

> I thought I should see Beatrice, and saw
> An old man, habited like the glorious people;
> O'er flowing was he, in his eyes and cheeks
> With joys benign, in attitude of piety,
> As to a tender father is becoming.

Later, Bernard teaches Dante to look beyond Beatrice, even beyond the Virgin Mary, to the One beyond:

> Bernard conveyed to me what I should do
> By sign and smile; already on my own
> I had looked upwards, as he wished me to.

"The knowledge of God and of one's self must come first, for they are essential to salvation....Know yourself and you will have a wholesome fear of God. Know God and you will also love God" (Sermon 37, I. II).

Our Experience

When the Greek way of thinking and Greek philosophy —especially that of Aristotle—were imported into medieval Europe via Turkey, they brought in their wake huge problems for Christianity, and not least for Christian spirituality.

The Greek conceptions of knowledge and love were completely alien to the Judeo-Christian mind. The Hebrew language knows very little of the abstract: its strength is in its verbs and its nouns, which are always concrete and substantial. Consequently, the Jew did not pursue philosophy, but rather religion, and essentially a religion concerned with a God of history.

Because the Hebrew vocabulary tolerates only one word for love, all love is of a piece. The Jewish language would not speak of "spiritual love" as opposed to "sexual love," and if Christianity, especially in the West, had stayed in closer contact with its Jewish roots, we would not have suffered dualism, and Freud would have been rendered redundant before he had ever put pen to paper.

For we should not divide love into good love and bad love depending upon what kind of love it is. Rather, all love is good or bad, depending upon the object to which it is directed. Hence, we should not speak so much of good love and bad love, but rather of appropriate and inappropriate love. The vision of God teaches us that ultimately all love should be directed to God and, through God, to God's creatures.

In the medieval collect adapted by Cranmer, the church prayed that we might love God "in all things and above all things." The problem began when Cranmer adapted this prayer to ask that we might love God simply "above all things." The inevitable question then arose: "What about all these other creatures I love so much?" "Well," replied Puritan Protestantism, "so long as you love them with pure, platonic, spiritual love, perhaps that will be more or less all right!"

Hence the schizoid world of love which we observe today. For St. Bernard, love was all of a piece—it was purely and simply love. In the unity of his doctrine of love, Bernard and all the saints found a unity for all their creative energies and a wholesome love permeating a healthy, holy life. We must seek to do the same whether married, widowed, celibate, or single.

WEEK FOUR: FRIDAY

Now Peter and John were going up to the temple at the hour of prayer, the ninth hour. And a man lame from birth was being carried, whom they laid daily at that gate of the temple which is called Beautiful to ask alms of those who entered the temple. Seeing Peter and John about to go into the temple, he asked for alms. And Peter directed his gaze at him, with John, and said, "Look at us." And he fixed his attention upon them, expecting to receive something from them. But Peter said, "I have no silver and gold, but I give you what I have; in the name of Jesus Christ of Nazareth, walk." And he took him by the right hand and raised him up; and immediately his feet and ankles were made strong. And leaping up he stood and walked and entered the temple with them, walking

and leaping and praising God. And all the people saw
him walking and praising God, and recognized him as
the one who sat for alms at the Beautiful Gate of the temple and they were filled with wonder and amazement at
what had happened to him. (Acts 3:1–10)

The Witness of Scripture

The book of Acts is Luke's continuing account of all that
Jesus did. The only difference between volume one (the
Gospel narrative) and volume two (Acts) is that in volume
two Jesus is carrying on his work through the hands of the
apostles, who have been anointed with the power of the
Holy Spirit.

On the way to the Temple, where the first Christians continued to go for their worship, Peter and John are accosted,
as Jesus frequently was, by someone in need—a beggar. The
man *wants* money: he *needs* Jesus. Fortunately, Peter does
not have any money, otherwise he might have been tempted
to fob the poor beggar off with small change. Yet, Peter has
something much more powerful to offer than merely small
change. He has the healing power of the risen, ascended
Lord to give to this poor man. And so Peter did what he had
seen Jesus doing on many occasions. We are told, by Dr.
Luke, that he "took him by the right hand" and "raised him
up." After all, Peter and John were now in the resurrection
business! Dr. Luke tells us that Peter had caught the habit of
offering a helping hand from Jesus, and that this was not
only a miraculous healing, but also part of that bigger picture of renewal and resurrection. (The word in Greek for
"raised up" deliberately has the same root as the word for
"resurrection.") Furthermore, the beggar did not just walk
anywhere. He followed Peter and John, as they had first followed Jesus. In a word, the man became a "disciple," and a
joyful disciple at that, leaping and jumping for joy in fulfillment of the messianic prophecy in Isaiah, "Then shall the
lame man leap like a hart." The man's healing is complete
because he became a disciple. He received both the Giver
and the gifts into his life.

Of course, this was the kind of evidence that healing,

renewal, and resurrection really do work; and it was the kind of evidence also that the Pharisees and the Sanhedrin found difficult to counter.

The Witness of the Saints

SAINT FRANCIS OF ASSISI (ca. 1181–1226)

Seduced by the glitter, the spectacular and the superficial, intoxicated by the world around him, and driven by the love within him, St. Francis of Assisi, the world's most popular saint, did not find the road to freedom in mediocrity, the norm, or the average. He was at all times an extremist for God and strove first to be possessed by him in order that he might repossess himself and then own afresh the world in all its beauty and simplicity. In order to do this, he must first be free of all possessions.

As a prosperous young man, he was captivated by the glitter of the world, by chivalry, romance, money (which he spent lavishly), clothes, and the glamor of the battlefield. In a word, he worshiped the creature rather than the Creator. Born the son of a wealthy cloth merchant of Assisi in 1181 or 1182, he was called Francis because much of his father's dealings took place in France. In fact, his father was in France at the time of the birth of his son.

Not at all interested in the tedium of his father's business, Francis enlisted in the army at the age of twenty or so, was captured prisoner, and held in captivity for a year. Somewhere between the end of 1203 and 1206, he became seriously ill and was subsequently converted to faith. He had several visions and "visitations" from the Lord at this time and undertook a pilgrimage to Rome to the tomb of St. Peter. He had turned full circle in his life; facing now a new direction, he saw the creature and the Creator in a new light. He was determined to leave behind him the worship of the creation and ruthlessly to seek the worship of the Creator.

For this he needed to strip himself of everything—clothes (literally), money, ambition, and worldly pomp—and so be ready to help the Lord to rebuild his church, not with the world's resources, nor motivated, as before, by the glorification of humankind, but "for the love of Christ's poor and the Crucified."

Once again, it was the living word of Scripture which redirected the life of Francis. He was attending Mass in the Church of San Damiano, a church which the little saint had rebuilt with his own hands. The church stands in a plain just two miles from Assisi. It was the feast of St. Matthias in the year 1209. The gospel appointed for the eucharist that day was Matthew 10:7–9: "Preach as you go, saying, 'The kingdom of heaven is at hand'....You have received without paying, give without pay. Take no gold, nor silver...nor two tunics, nor sandals, nor a staff." So he took Jesus at his word, and Jesus took hold of St. Francis in that moment and marked him for life. Francis applied those words of the gospel directly to himself. He gave away his shoes, his staff, and his girdle, and left himself only with one poor coat, tied around his middle with a cord. This was to become the dress of his friars—the undyed woolen dress of the shepherds and peasants in those parts. So it was that he fell in love with the world again, but this time because he had first found the love of God its Creator.

There was nothing of the Puritan about Francis.

He kissed the hand of a leper; he loved the poor; he loved the natural world around him—birds, wolves, sun, and moon—and even what he called "Sister Bodily Death."

Yes, "marked for life!" On Holy Cross Day (September 14), just two years before he died, while engaged in prayer, in a little cell on Mount Alvernia where he had withdrawn with Brother Leo, he had his most powerful vision of Christ crucified and subsequently received the stigmata in his hands and feet and side. St. Clare, his lifelong friend in the Lord, nursed him for six weeks on his death bed. On October 3, 1226, Francis died as he lived, in absolute humility and total poverty, naked and on the naked earth.

St. Francis of Assisi, the revolutionary and freedom fighter, found true worship for the true God and it was that which set him free to love the world for Christ with a passion closer to our Lord's own passion than that experienced by almost any saint God has ever given to the world.

Our Experience

In the history of iconography, there are recurring chapters of decadence in which the icon, which is intended to be
a window into glory, glorifies itself with jewels and excessive decoration encrusted over the icon. So the icon, which
is always intended to point beyond itself and become a means
to an end, draws attention to itself and becomes an end in itself. Thus, the icon of one generation is always in danger of
becoming the idol of the next generation. At that point there
is a necessary iconoclastic movement that ruthlessly tears
down the icon that has become an idol and demands that
absolutely nothing, not even the church, can ever come between us and the life of God in Christ Jesus our Lord.

> The dearest idol I have known,
> What 'ere that idol be:
> Oh, help me tear it from thy throne,
> And worship only thee.
>
> (William Cowper)

So we can see how each and every generation must pray
and work for the renewal and rebuilding of Christ's church.
Renewal is a recurring theme in the history of the church, for
the church is intended to be an icon and is perpetually in danger of degenerating into an idol. I must love the church because it is the mother of my faith, yet I should learn to love
the church most when it talks most about Jesus and least
about itself. The church is not an end in itself; its work is to
point continually beyond itself to the kingdom. In the heavenly Jerusalem of Revelation there is no temple. Furthermore, all the analogies which Jesus gives us for the church
in the New Testament—salt, light, and leaven—are images
that essentially point beyond themselves. Salt is lost in a
well-flavored dish in which it brings out the taste, not of itself, but of the food which is salted and flavored. Good
lighting illuminates and should not draw attention to itself,
otherwise it is by definition bad lighting. Leaven is lost in
the lump.

St. Francis was a rich young man who loved beautiful
things. Yet, he refused to let anything get in the way of a life
directed toward and lived for the glory of God, for His own

sake. Only so was he able to be obedient to his vision and rebuild Christ's church. At the outset of the apostolic ministry, in the book of Acts, we should note how Peter tells the beggar that he has no silver or gold, but indeed that he does have something far more precious to give to that beggar—a knowledge of God's love in the person of Jesus as Savior and Lord. A church which is rich in goods will nearly always be poor in holiness and faith and generally ineffective in evangelism. Nearly always, when people ask us for money, we should be very careful not to sell them short by just giving them money. We all have far deeper needs than financial ones, which something far richer than riches alone can satisfy.

In an age which has witnessed the swift demise of Communism in Russia, the West should know that there is now a real spiritual vacuum in the life of that great civilization. Perestroika (renewal) in Russia constitutes a spiritual challenge to the materialism and hedonism of the West, for if we have nothing to offer to a bankrupt Russia except weary, decadent capitalism, then indeed, the world is in real peril.

Francis recalled the church of his day to spiritual renewal, because his own life had first been renewed and recaptured by the love of God for God's own sake. Only so were things that had been cast down in the thirteenth century able to be raised up, and things that had grown old were able to be made new. In a word, Jesus was worshiped again as Lord of his church, for until our Lord is Lord of all, he is not really Lord at all. According to John's Gospel, it is only when Jesus is glorified that the Holy Spirit is given and authentic renewal can truly begin. We need another St. Francis in our day, in order that God might rebuild his church to be an effective instrument for the conversion and evangelization of the world of the twenty-first century.

WEEK FOUR: SATURDAY

Now there was at Joppa a disciple named Tabitha, which means Dorcas. She was full of good works and acts of charity. In those days she fell sick and died; and when they had washed her, they laid her in an upper room.

Since Lydda was near Joppa, the disciples, hearing that Peter was there, sent two men to him entreating him, "Please come down to us without delay." So Peter rose and went with them. And when he had come, they took him to the upper room. All the widows stood beside him weeping, and showing tunics and other garments which Dorcas made while she was with them. But Peter put them all outside and knelt down and prayed; then turning to the body he said, "Tabitha, rise." And she opened her eyes, and when she saw Peter she sat up. And he gave her his hand and lifted her up. Then calling the saints and widows he presented her alive. And it became known throughout all Joppa, and many believed in the Lord. (Acts 9:36–42)

The Witness of Scripture

In the ministry of healing and renewal, we are all called by our baptism not only to *imitate* Jesus to others, but to *be* Jesus for others. In this story of the raising of Tabitha, we see Peter acting so closely on behalf of Christ as his apostle, that his very words and actions are almost identical with those that Peter had seen and heard during the earthly ministry of Jesus.

Only a few verses earlier than our story of Tabitha, Luke records the story of Peter's healing of an old, bedridden, paralyzed man. Peter speaks to him almost the same words that Jesus had said to that other paralyzed man in Capernaum: "Get up, take your mat and go home." Peter says to Aeneas, "Get up, and tidy up your mat." In both cases, the word used for "get up" is again that word for resurrection—"rise up!"

Then Peter is immediately called to Joppa to minister to the dead Tabitha. As in the gospel story of the raising of Jairus' daughter, so here again Peter finds, on his arrival, a great commotion, with widows wailing around the death bed. Taught by Jesus what to do, Peter turns them all out of the room, exactly as Jesus had done in the case of Jairus' daughter. Kneeling down by the bed, Peter then prays to Jesus. He then turns to the dead woman and says, "Tabitha, get up." If we assume that Peter said this in Aramaic, he would have said, "Tabitha, koum!" We know from the gospel account of the raising of Jairus' daughter that Jesus said on that occasion, "Talitha, koum!" "Little girl, get up." Notice, there is a difference of only one letter between the instruction of Peter and that of Jesus.

Renewal and resurrection are the ministry of the risen Lord through his church to his people. Most of us, most of the time, are only half alive. The Lord of life longs to bring us to that fullness of life through healing and daily renewal in his Holy Spirit, so that the works that he did once upon a time, and even "greater works," we may also continue to do all the time, to the end of time (John 14:12).

The Witness of the Saints

SAINT MARTIN OF TOURS (ca. 316–397)

St. Martin, a patron saint of France, was born in Pannonia, a town in Sabaria. His father, a pagan and an army officer, was called to service in Pavia, Italy, where Martin, while still only a boy of ten, chose on his own accord to become a catechumen. Five years later, he was compelled by his father against his own will to enlist in the Roman army. While stationed in Amiens, the famous incident occurred in which Martin gave his cloak to a beggar. It was during a particularly hard winter and a severe frost that Martin, on horseback, met at the gate of the city a beggar who was almost naked, "trembling and shaking with cold and begging alms of those that passed by." Martin, we are told, took off his great army cloak, cut it into two pieces, gave one half to the beggar and wrapped himself in the other half.

That night, Martin had a vision in which he saw Jesus dressed in the half of his cloak and saying, "Martin, yet a catechumen, has covered me with his garment." Next day, we are told by Martin's biographer, Martin "flew to be baptized."

Obtaining discharge from the army as a conscientious objector, which was not an easy undertaking, Martin went first to Milan and then to Illyricum. He was driven from both places by the Arians. In 360, he joined Bishop Hilary of Poitiers and founded the first monastery in Gaul at Liguge. In 372, Martin became bishop of Tours at the invitation of the local people and set about encouraging the spread of monasticism, himself leading at all times the simple life of a monk. As such, he evangelized the whole countryside and introduced a kind of rudimentary parochial system.

Martin's own life of simplicity and poverty, his care for the poor, and his work as a pastor in the healing ministry were all especially noteworthy attributes of his outstanding episcopate. He had received rudimentary medical training in the army, but added to this with the gift of Holy Orders; in those days a bishop was expected to "heal the sick" as well as to teach and preach. His ministry to the sick, the mentally ill, and the possessed are all well documented and were to form the basis of his ministry as a bishop. He died while visiting a remote part of his diocese on November 8, 397.

Our Experience

The ministry of healing, forgiveness, and reconciliation is central to our understanding of the full-blooded, catholic gospel of Jesus Christ. The pages of the New Testament leave us in no doubt that Jesus healed the sick and raised the dead. Furthermore, the promise of Jesus to his church is absolutely clear: "The works that I do you shall do and greater works than these, because I go to the Father" (John 14:12).

So his anointed, apostolic church is intended to continue that same saving, healing ministry, by imitating Christ in the power of the Spirit. Peter had learned that healing ministry from the Master Physician or Savior. The root word in Greek and Latin for salvation, saved, and Savior can also be translated as healing, healed, or Physician. Indeed, Tyndale in his English translation of the scriptures does precisely that, in such a way as to bring an holistic slant to Christian spirituality. In the New Testament understanding of ministry, all healing, forgiveness, salvation, and renewal are to be found in the same bundle—it is a package deal.

St. Martin learned how to cure the symptoms of illness in the medical corps of the Roman army. He learned how to heal the souls and bodies of men and women in the "salvation army" of Christ's apostolic church. In the early church, the bishop would be the first person to be called to the bedside of the sick and the dying—not the last person, when all other hope had gone! He would arrive, often with a choir to sing and also with oil for anointing (in obedience to the scriptural injunction in the epistle of James). For all sin brings disease, though we must not assume that the equation is reversible—sickness is not necessarily a sign that this particular person has sinned and caused the illness (John 9:3). Psychology, together with the personal ministry so closely associated with the renewal movements of the church, both remind us that sin and guilt bring disease and have made personal ministry and counseling much more accessible and acceptable than in the past.

Yet, there is a moment when counseling should cease and "gospeling" should begin; when prayer should be offered, confession of sins be invited, and absolution proclaimed and ministered, followed by laying on of hands, anointing with oil, and a specific prayer for healing of body, mind, and spirit.

One further point needs to be made. Often, when we are given the gift of healing and have been healed, it is also a sign that we need to go out and heal others. All gifts in the New Testament are given for the sake of the whole Body and are to be given away. For the apostolic figure in the church—like Peter and Martin—is always a wounded healer, who simply cannot restrain himself from speaking of the things he has "seen and heard" and, exactly like the alcoholic who has found sobriety, necessarily goes out to hand on to others that which he himself has first received. Peter was renewed, forgiven, raised up, and healed by Christ after breakfast on that resurrection morning by the lake of Tiberias (John 21). It was only a matter of weeks before he found himself out on the road healing others with Jesus as his model physician. So it was also with Martin of Tours. Jesus had come to him in the guise of the naked beggar so that Martin, in turn, might minister Jesus to others in evangelization and in a gospel ministry of healing, forgiveness, and renewal.

The Calling

And I heard the voice of the Lord saying, "Whom shall I send, and who will go for us?"

INTRODUCING WEEK FIVE

The disciple simply burns his boats and goes ahead. He is called out and has to forsake his old life in order that he may 'exist' in the strictest sense of the word. The old life is left behind, and completely surrendered. The disciple is dragged out of his relative security into a life of absolute insecurity (that is, in truth, in to the absolute security and safety of the fellowship of Jesus); from a life which is observable and calculable (it is, in fact, quite incalculable) into a life where everything is unobservable and fortuitous (that is, one which is necessary and calculable); out of the realm of finite (which is, in truth, the infinite) into the realm of infinite possibilities (which is the one liberating reality).

> (Dietrich Bonhoeffer: *The Cost of Discipleship*, SCM Press Ltd., 1959, p. 49)

Such is the paradox of the Christian vocation: "whose bondage is perfect freedom."

For the call is not to let go of the good for the less good, but rather to let go of the good for the better and the best. Furthermore, what we possessed in fact possessed us. Luke tells us that Peter, on the day of his call, was mending his nets. The trouble was that he was doing that every day. If he was not mending them, he was washing them; and if he was not washing and mending them, he was breaking them and then having to wash and mend them all over again. Peter was netted in his own nets. Instead of fishing to live, he was now living to fish—and apparently he was not doing any of

137

this too well on the day that Jesus called him.

So often, we need to be set free from our talents and our enthusiasms, not because they make us too happy, but because they cannot give us what in the end will really make us happy enough. For the joy is not to be found in any of these pursuits in themselves, but rather in the joy that comes to us through them. And it is the voice of the Caller, calling in and through the things of this world that, in turn, makes us so very homesick for heaven.

Even the best of everything else is only "the echo of a tune we have not heard; the scent of a flower we have not yet picked and news from a country we have not yet visited" (C.S. Lewis). We shall only get to that country of promise and gift if we follow step by step behind Jesus who has gone ahead to prepare a place. Yet, in order to be ultimately attached, we shall need at some point to be detached from that which still binds us to this earth.

So the call of Christ is intended to dislocate the whole human race and to save us from settling for the best that this world has to give: making the best of a bad job, as we so often lamentably say. The call of Christ should disturb us in our sleep, in our complacence, and in our indifference. Essentially, it must move us, physically as well as emotionally and in every other way. It must bring us to our feet after it has first brought us to our knees—hands outstretched and all eyes on him, who has set his face now towards the heavenly Jerusalem, where he ever lives to make intercession for us.

Questions for Personal Reflection or Discussion in Groups

1. In what practical ways can we implement the full implication of a doctrine that teaches that all baptized Christians are called to ministry? Is there any discipleship which does not involve ministry?

2. In what ways can we test the call of God to see whether we are deluded or mistaken?

3. Is there an overlapping between natural inclination, talents, and traits on the one hand, and the calling of God

into his service on the other? If so, what does that tell us about our own calling into discipleship and service?

4. Let us resolve to read and study the lives of the saints so that we can learn to see the hand of God at work in the lives of his chosen people.

WEEK FIVE: MONDAY

Now the Lord said to Abram, "Go from your country and your kindred and your father's house to the land that I will show you. And I will make of you a great nation, and I will bless you, and make your name great, so that you will be a blessing. I will bless those who bless you, and him who curses you I will curse; and by you all the families of the earth shall bless themselves."

So Abram went, as the Lord had told him; and Lot went with him. Abram was seventy-five years old when he departed from Haran. And Abram took Sarai his wife, and Lot his brother's son, and all their possessions which they had gathered, and the persons that they had gotten in Haran; and they set forth to go to the land of Canaan. (Gen. 12:1–5)

The Witness of Scripture

Adam grasped at the tree of knowledge, and in so doing closed off that way of knowledge for the whole human race. Abraham is the father of a new way. He is the father of a new kind of knowledge—a knowledge which comes through faith and is summarized in the phrase, "I believe, in order that I may understand."

So, at a great age, the old man leaves all that he has known for the unknown and sets out *not knowing* where he is going. In one sense it is foolishness, and certainly Sarah and Lot and all the other hangers on must have continually said so. He is swapping possessions for promises and that which is certain for that which only may be. Yet, this is to be the new way forward for humanity. It is the way that human history has developed ever since. We have our working hypotheses which we assume are true, but we cannot prove them to be true unless we act on the assumption that they are true. Faith, then, is a hunch—all this can only be proved, like that proverbial pudding, simply in the eating.

And God is the God of Abraham, whom we can only come to know by responding in faith and trust to that call originally given to Abraham. The echo of that call is in the heart of every man, woman, and child. So we are asked not to settle for what we have, but rather to go out in faith to receive what God has promised still to give us. Only so shall we come out of darkness into light; from the land of possessions to the land of gift and promise.

The Witness of the Saints

SAINT SERGIUS (ca.1314–92)

St. Sergius was the outstanding and most highly regarded abbot of his age, and has remained so throughout the history of the Russian Orthodox Church. Not only laymen, from peasants to princes, but also bishops, priests, and clergy of all ranks, as well as monks and bishops from other monasteries came to visit him and to be advised by him.

St. Sergius had many visions in his lifetime. One of them at least proved to be prophetic. He saw many flying birds. A voice said, "Sergius, the Lord has accepted your prayer. Your disciples who come after you will be as many as the multitude of these birds."

The second son of Rostov nobles, Cyril and Maria, Bartholomew—as Sergius was first called—was a very religious boy and was inclined to the monastic life from the outset. Yet, to start with, he was rather backward and a somewhat retarded boy, unable to read or work with books. On the death of his parents, Bartholomew accompanied his eldest brother Stephen to a nearby forest outside Radonezh, not far from Moscow. Stephen was not able to bear the hardships and emptiness of the vast northern forest and so left his younger brother to the solitary life while he went to a monastery in Moscow city.

It was not long before the solitary Sergius began to attract disciples. Gradually he received twelve novices. In

1354, Sergius was ordained to the priesthood, forming a monastic community with himself as the abbot.

Life in St. Sergius' monastery was exceedingly austere from the very outset. Instead of wax candles, wooden torches were used; vestments were of the simplest colored linen and the sacred vessels were made only of wood; often there was nothing to eat for two or three days at a time.

Like so many contemplatives and solitaries, Sergius was called upon to be involved in those very things from which he had so earnestly sought freedom and release. At the Holy Trinity monastery, in spite of all his outside concerns in state and church, Sergius was still able to reestablish authentic monastic community life—a pattern of life which had been lost in Russia through the Tartar invasion.

His influence over all classes was enormous. He stopped four civil wars between Russian princes and supported and inspired the resistance of Prince Dimitri, which in turn saved Russia from further Tartar invasions (1380).

Although St. Alexius, the Russian primate, wanted Sergius to succeed him as patriarch, Sergius declined the honor. Altogether it is reckoned that during his lifetime he founded some forty monasteries. Canonized very soon after his death, St. Sergius is beyond serious dispute the patron saint of Russia.

Our Experience

The word "ecclesiastical" is derived from the Latin word for the church—*ecclesia*—and its root meaning denotes a group of people who have been "called out" of one environment into a new and different environment. In other words, the church is a group of "displaced persons," or better still, perhaps a group of "resident aliens." Again and again in the Old Testament, God calls his people out of their natural environment, displacing them, uprooting them, and moving them to an alien environment. It began with old Abraham, who had settled down in his old age. Suddenly he is uprooted and called by God to go very late in life to a foreign land to start another, quite different sort of life. God calls him to leave the known for the unknown, and security for maturity. Yahweh needs to wean his people from their household gods and from the inevitable pantheism that dominates in a culture rooted in the land. The old Israel needed to become a nomadic, pilgrim people.

So when Sergius left the city, the known, and the secure for the forest and the unknown, he became in a real sense part of God's displaced people as he went to the "laboratory" of solitude where he could learn for himself that God is indeed the provider of all that we really need. He set out on that journey through the desert to the land of gift and of promise.

For the new Israel, the church, the calling out of God's people continues and is just as important. "Our commonwealth is in heaven," says St. Paul. Christians are homesick for heaven, and their spirituality and lifestyle should show it in many different ways. Christians are called out to stand out. The Christian pilgrim should never feel quite at home in this world—a sort of square peg in a round hole! Or, to use another image, a Christian living the life of heaven on earth should perhaps feel a bit like a bull in a china shop. Bulls were not made for delicate, claustrophobic china shops, after all, but rather for the wide open spaces. So in the same way, human beings were not made for this world—we were made for heaven, and we shall never really feel at home until we are there. In the meantime, Christian faith communities pursue a common lifestyle, sharing their riches and their spiritual and material gifts as they learn to live in increasing dependence upon a God who has graciously bestowed upon them their daily bread and all the necessary resources for that fullness of life which can only be fully lived in heaven, our real and lasting home.

WEEK FIVE: TUESDAY

> At that time Eli, whose eyesight had begun to grow dim, so that he could not see, was lying down in his own place; the lamp of God had not yet gone out, and Samuel was lying down within the temple of the Lord, where the ark of God was. Then the Lord called, "Samuel! Samuel!" and

he said, "Here I am!" and ran to Eli, and said, "Here I am, for you called me." But he said, "I did not call; lie down again." So he went and lay down. And the Lord called again, "Samuel!" And Samuel arose and went to Eli, and said, "Here I am, for you called me." But he said, "I did not call, my son; lie down again." Now Samuel did not yet know the Lord, and the word of the Lord had not yet been revealed to him. And the Lord called Samuel again the third time. And he arose and went to Eli, and said, "Here I am, for you called me." Then Eli perceived that the Lord was calling the boy. Therefore Eli said to Samuel, "Go, lie down; and if he calls you, you shall say, "Speak, Lord, for thy servant hears." So Samuel went and lay down in his place.

And the Lord came and stood forth, calling as at other times, "Samuel! Samuel!" And Samuel said, "Speak, for thy servant hears." (1 Sam. 3:2–10)

The Witness of Scripture

Samuel was the child of gift to Hannah—a name which itself means gift or grace. For all life is a gift.

Hannah gives back her gifted child, Samuel, to the Lord. Yet, so far Samuel has had no say in all of this. At some point, sooner or later, Samuel must become personally involved in this whole transaction of grace. Our faith and our calling are never individualistic, but they are certainly personal. All sorts of people are corporately involved in what we like to call a personal faith—we must not make the mistake, however, of calling it an individual faith.

So, "Samuel did not yet know the Lord"—he only had secondhand knowledge through the faith and witness of others. In his call, that secondhand faith of Samuel would become a truly personal and firsthand encounter with the living God.

Eli's faith, on the other hand, had grown dim. The author of this book is intent upon telling us, literally and metaphorically, that the lamp of God had not yet gone out in the darkened temple. From time to time in the history of the church, the lamp of faith grows dim and the church grows dark. At such times, God calls out his saints and rekindles the fire of their faith. Yet, all that is gift, too.

God calls in the darkness of the temple to Samuel by name, and invites the boy to walk into the future which God has prepared for him, so that the future which God longs to prepare for the whole of Israel may indeed come to pass. Samuel is called out, not for privilege in his nation, but for service. He is called out as a prophet to recall God's people to renewal in faith and discipleship.

The Witness of the Saints

SAINT JOAN OF ARC (1412–31)

"God sent a voice to guide me," said Sainte Jeanne la Pucelle, or Joan of Arc as English-speaking people insist upon calling her. "At first I was very much frightened. The voice came towards the hour of noon, in summer, in my father's garden. I had fasted the previous day. I heard the voice on my right hand, in the direction of the church. I seldom hear it without seeing a light. That light always appears on the side from which I hear the voice."

Just a young girl in her teens at that time, Joan was born at Domrémy, on the feast of the Epiphany, in a little village in the Champagne country. She was one of five children. Voices and visions were to stay with her all though her brief and tumultuous life.

By the time Joan was seventeen, the voices had become insistent and explicit. She was to leave home and to seek out Robert Beaudricourt, who commanded the king's forces in the Champagne country. Traveling in male dress and escorted by three men at arms, on March 6, 1429, she was admitted to see the king, Charles, whom she managed to convince of her divine mission. On May 8 of that same year, with an army under her command, she was able to drive the English from Orleans and went on to crush the English at Patay. On July 17, Charles was solemnly crowned king of France in Rheims cathedral with Joan standing at his side, with her special standard bearing the words "Jesus: Maria"—the standard under which she had led France to victory.

The crowning of the king marked the end of Joan's successful military campaign. Betrayed by the French and sold to the English later that year, she was tried as a sorceress and as a heretic.

During the course of six public and nine shameful sessions, Joan was examined and cross-examined about her visions and her voices; about her persistence in wearing male attire; about her faith, and her willingness to submit to the church. The trial was highly motivated throughout by political considerations.

At one point, she withdrew her claim to the validity of the voices and submitted to the church. Shortly afterwards, however, she turned again, claiming that the voices of St. Catherine and St. Margaret had upbraided her for her "revocation to save" her life, and that in thus seeking to save her life, she was damning herself for eternity.

On Tuesday, May 29, 1431, the judges condemned her as a relapsed heretic, and on the following morning, the English burned Joan, age only nineteen, at the stake.

Very much the patron saint of France, Joan of Arc defies any straightforward human assessment. It simply will not do to try to pigeon-hole her into twentieth-century causes or Freudian or Jungian categories, or to see her as a feminist before her time, or to use any other plausible slogan to seek to rationalize what is clearly an amazing, shocking, and yet quite remarkable life. Like all the saints, Joan of Arc, in the last analysis remains a mystery which will only make sense when all our senses are finally subsumed and enfolded into the ultimate mystery of God—our Creator, redeemer, and sanctifier.

In fact, it was not until 1920 that the church canonized Joan and recognized her formally as a saint. In order to do so the church necessarily had to swallow its own words by which it had formally condemned her as a heretic. The same church that condemned her, eventually canonized her. Such is the paradox and the contradiction of the saints in every age!

Our Experience

Voices are as distinctive as features and as unique as fingerprints for those "with ears to hear." When we answer the telephone, we can nearly always recognize the caller by their voice, and furthermore, the absence of visual characteristics on a telephone means that our sense of hearing is more intense, so that we are more sensitive to the tone of the voice at the other end and can often tell whether the caller is tired, annoyed, happy, or rather flat.

The voice of God is equally distinctive for those "with ears to hear." We are told that little Samuel did not yet "know the Lord." He had not yet learned to distinguish the voice of God. Therefore, Samuel confuses the voice of God with the voice of Eli, the old patriarchal figure.

We live in an age of words and mass communication. How on earth, we might well ask, are we to learn to hear the voice of God and his call and to recognize that call amidst the cacophony of the many competitive words, sounds, and noises of our contemporary world? Certainly we should not try to pretend to have some hot line to God. Certainly for most of us, God speaks *through* the words and sounds and lights of everyday life. So we must first learn to know God's word *somewhere*, before we shall be able to recognize his voice and his word *anywhere*. Samuel did not yet know the Lord, so how could he have recognized God's voice and God's words?

Yet, we must come in some sense to know the Lord, his ways, and his words. In order to do that, we must study *the* revelation of his word so that we shall be able to spot and recognize other revelations when we see or hear them. It is only as we come to know God's holy word, his call, his voice, and his presence in Scripture and in the sacraments that we can become more and more aware of his living word and his presence in and through the words and features of everyday life. "The Word became flesh" and has continued to do so, embodied in the most unlikely and surprising tones, features, and guises, so that we often entertain angels and messengers unawares, as little Samuel did.

So we need to pray to the Holy Spirit for that precious gift of discernment. At the same time we must not forget that the devil masquerades as the angel of light and can imitate God's voice and even use God's word for his own ends, as he did with Jesus in the wilderness temptations.

Yet, it is only in prayer and in silence, as we study God's known word and revelation and his call to his people in times past, that we can more easily recognize that same word through the words of the preacher, as we read "between the lines" of the daily news, of as we increasingly see God's hand in "the words of the prophets, written on the subway walls"—so that heaven and earth come alive with the "sounds of silence," the echoes of God's voice and the traces of his glory.

WEEK FIVE: WEDNESDAY

Now the word of the Lord came to me saying, "Before I formed you in the womb I knew you, and before you were born I consecrated you; I appointed you a prophet to the nations." Then I said, "Ah, Lord God! Behold, I do not know how to speak, for I am only a youth." But the Lord said to me, "Do not say, 'I am only a youth'; for to all to whom I send you shall go, and whatever I command you you shall speak. Be not afraid of them, for I am with you to deliver you, says the Lord." Then the Lord put forth his hand and touched my mouth; and the Lord said to me, "Behold, I have put my words in your mouth. See, I have set you this day over nations and over kingdoms, to pluck up and to break down, to destroy and to overthrow, to build and to plant." (Jer. 1:4–10)

The Witness of Scripture

So that we may be quite certain that we cannot qualify to be called, we need to know that God has called his people from before time, and before he formed us in the womb. Furthermore, we did not choose him, but rather he chose us, even before we were conceived. Such is always the work of what we call prevenient grace.

The work of the preacher and the prophet alike are both the work of God. Notice that the prophet feels singularly ill equipped for his call. He is not eloquent by nature, and he is only a youth with very little past experience.

So a response to the call is only possible because God

has retained and will retain the initiative throughout the whole of Jeremiah's ministry. "Whom he calls, he empowers" (Anselm). Jeremiah is only to go where God sends him, and he is only to speak the word of the Lord, which is not the same as giving his own opinions, however well informed! Jeremiah's ministry will be both destructive and constructive—here is no smooth message, but rather a dynamic message!

And all this is possible only because Jeremiah's preaching will be anointed. The Lord touches the mouth and lips of the prophet, both to cleanse and to anoint. Such is the stuff of which great preachers, teachers, and prophets have been made throughout the ages. It is all the Lord's doing "and it is marvelous in our eyes."

So Paul, when moving from Athens to Corinth, had learned this basic lesson. He writes from bitter experience after the "flop" of his preaching in Athens, where he founded no church at all. "When I came to you, brethren, I did not come proclaiming to you the testimony of God in lofty words or wisdom. For I decided to know nothing among you except Jesus Christ and him crucified. And I was with you in weakness and in much fear and trembling; and my speech and my message were not plausible words of wisdom, but in demonstration of the spirit and of power, that your faith might not rest in the wisdom of men but in the power of God" (1 Cor. 2:1-5).

The Witness of the Saints

SAINT DOMINIC (1170–1221)

Preaching for conversion of mind, heart, and life–that was the mandate handed to Dominic by the Lord. At the beginning of his life, Dominic's vocation was fostered through the Order of Regular Canons of St. Augustine, and he followed that rule assiduously. However, he saw that something was lacking in that order. He "earnestly desired to revive an apostolic spirit in the ministers of the altar." Dominic saw with a passionate clarity the need to "unite contemplation with a close application to sacred studies and all the functions of a pastoral life," but "especially that of preaching."

In Dominic's day, the Albigensians dominated huge areas of Europe. Dominic sharpened the tongue of his apologetics and gave his energies to preaching about this new sect, especially in Languedoc. In order to win souls for Christ, Dominic was adamant that the preacher's life must be in accordance with gospel priorities and especially committed to poverty and simplicity of lifestyle.

So the Rule which confirmed his Order of Preachers, when taken to Rome in 1216, for confirmation by the Pope, outlined the spirituality of the preacher. He was to be itinerant and copy the poverty of friars and the whole Franciscan spirit. Learning and study, as well as a special commitment to the preached word, were to be an important part of the life.

As soon as his order and its constitutions were confirmed by Pope Honorius III, after instituting his little band of Dominicans, he immediately broke them up and dispersed them in all directions. Four were sent to Spain, seven to Paris, and two to Toulouse, while Dominic returned to Rome, where he ministered in the church of St. Sixtus (San Sisto Vecchio). He preached with great power in Rome, formed a community of nuns, and established two strong Dominican centers in the universities of Paris and Bologna.

The Order of Preachers grew remarkably in Spain, France and Italy in Dominic's lifetime, and by the second General Chapter in 1221 it had no less than sixty friaries divided into eight provinces scattered across Poland, Scandinavia, and Palestine. Dominic died in Bologna on August 6, 1221, at the age of fifty-two.

Our Experience

How does God call us to his service? St. Paul puts the argument most clearly.

"How are men to call upon him in whom they have not believed? And how are they to believe in him of whom they have never heard? And how are they to hear without a preacher? And how can men preach unless they are sent?"

(Rom. 10:14–15). So in every generation, God calls some
people to preach his holy word and to proclaim the gospel
message. There is no living church without an apostolic
preacher. Today more than ever, we need to pray that God
will raise up preachers of his holy word—messengers of the
gospel, men and women in whose mouths he places his precious word of life. For as in Dominic's day, we live at a time
of conflicting religions and of false prophets. God's people
need to be fed and nourished with his word, in Bible study
as well as from the pulpit.

Like Mary, the mother of the Lord, and like Jeremiah in
the Old Testament, all baptized Christians are called to be
bearers of God's word within them. A Christian should literally embody God's word. Dominic taught his brethren to
love and to cherish the word of God. In anglicanism we
pray to God that, by his Holy Spirit, we might "read, mark,
learn and inwardly digest" the word of God, so that his
word may be formed in us and engrafted into our hearts
and into our subconscious. Then that word will be very near
to us at all times, on our lips because it is first in our hearts.
Then we shall be able to share the word of God with others,
and they will be enabled to hear God's call to them from our
lips, because we have first accepted him and his call in our
hearts. Furthermore, we can use that same word of God to
confront evil and to unmask the devil, as Jesus did when he
was tempted in the wilderness. Three times he refuted the
false call of Satan with a text from Scripture. For "all scripture is inspired by God and profitable for teaching, for re-
proof, for correction, and for training in righteousness, that
the man of God may be complete, equipped for every good
work" (2 Tim. 3:16–17).

WEEK FIVE: THURSDAY

As Jesus passed on from there, he saw a man called
Matthew sitting at the tax office; and he said to him, "Follow me." And he rose and followed him.

And as he sat at table in the house, behold, many tax
collectors and sinners came and sat down with Jesus and

his disciples. And when the Pharisees saw this, they said to his disciples, "Why does your teacher eat with tax collectors and sinners?" But when he heard it, he said, "Those who are well have no need of a physician, but those who are sick. Go and learn what this means, 'I desire mercy, and not sacrifice.' For I came not to call the righteous, but sinners." (Matthew 9:9–13)

The Witness of Scripture

It is most interesting to note that the call of Matthew is recorded in all three Synoptic Gospels. In both Mark and Luke, however, Matthew's old name, Levi, is used; and only in Matthew's Gospel—almost certainly written by Matthew—is the new name of Matthew used at all. Levi means, in Hebrew, "he who cleaves to the old ways." On the other hand, Matthew in translation means "the gift of Jehovah."

Matthew's call constitutes a move from the old conservative man with his grasping and cautious ways to the new man who is learning to love by gift under the grace and generosity of God. The difference is between night and day. The call of Matthew is recorded briefly and with little or no background. Could it be that Matthew had already heard some of the teachings of Jesus as he sat in his booth, pursuing his thankless task and his ill-gotten gains? He might have heard Jesus tell that story of the tax collector and the Pharisee who went up into the temple to pray. In any event, the two simple words—"Follow me"—were apparently enough to do the trick.

That very evening, Matthew, the new man, extended generous hospitality to Jesus and his friends. The Pharisees had a rule that they would never eat with tax collectors, or publicans, as they are sometimes called in the New Testament. However, the word soon got around about the great party that old Levi had given. So the Pharisees challenged Jesus. Jesus in his reply made the call of God quite explicit. He told the Pharisees quite plainly that God came to call sinners, not the self-righteous, into partnership with him to work for the kingdom.

It is sinners, then, who are the first to receive the call, for it is sinners, rather than the self-righteous who have settled down to a complacent and self-satisfied lifestyle, who are most likely to know their need of God. Again, however, we need to know how truly shocked the religious leaders are with the company that Jesus is keeping and with the kind of people he is calling to be his disciples and apostles. And, in one sense, they had every reason to be so shocked. We should not be too certain that we would not have been equally shocked on that day when Jesus chose and called old Levi, out of all the people in town that day, to be new Matthew. Surely he was the least likely, humanly speaking, to be called to be a disciple and one of the Twelve. Yet, Jesus knew and could see what the religious cronies could not see. Possessed by his possessions, Matthew had a great longing to belong. Jesus speaks to that longing and yearning in Matthew, as he always speaks to the old sinner who is potentially a "new" saint in the remaking.

The Witness of the Saints

JOSEPHINE BUTLER (1828–1907)

Returning from a party one evening to their home in Cheltenham, the Reverend George Butler and his wife Josephine were enthusiastically welcomed by their excited children—three sons and their six-year old daughter Eva, the "light and joy of their hearts." Little Eva was eager to be the first to greet her parents. Running to meet them, she fell head first over the banister of the large staircase in the entrance to their home and was killed immediately.

It was not incidental, therefore, that, later in life, Josephine Butler should emphasize the place of suffering and prayer in effective work and witness for God. In the years of grief and bereavement that followed upon the tragic death of little Eva, Josephine Butler discovered a call to meet and comfort people more unhappy than herself. It had been an old Quaker lady, in fact, who had told Josephine to go out and to look for new "daughters" amidst the miseries of the great seaport town of Liverpool, where her husband had been appointed as principal of the college in 1865.

So began Josephine's life and work for the poor, the abused, the prostitutes, and the oppressed. At first, she simply took several young women and girls to live in her overlarge house. Then she worked to deliver countless poor and working-class women from the monstrous implications of the new Acts for the Prevention of Contagious Diseases. Under these acts, plainclothed policemen were empowered to arrest and bring before a magistrate any woman whom they had "good cause" to believe to be a common prostitute.

Although her husband, a clergyman of the Church of England, strongly supported her, Josephine received very little support and much opposition from church leaders, Prime Minister Gladstone, and the Liberal Party, who were then in power. She wrote pamphlets, traveled as an itinerant speaker and lecturer (often in the face of great personal danger), and eventually succeeded in overturning the Acts for the Prevention of Contagious Diseases; she raised the age of consent to sixteen and did much to prevent and reduce child abuse and child prostitution, which were so prevalent in England and Europe at the end of the Victorian era.

But in all of this, she was first and foremost a woman of prayer and the spiritual life. "We have worked, we have slaved for duty, we have worn ourselves out in the service of humanity," she wrote later in life. "That is good and that is noble. Yet an inward voice will tell us that we should have worked better and served humanity more had we possessed the moral force to withdraw at times from life's crowdedness in order that our speech and our actions might have possessed more of the divine, more of the spirit of life."

Her suffering in early life opened her and enlarged her heart for the way of the contemplative. When Oscar Wilde was disgraced and in prison, she wrote, "I am so sorry for him. I long to be allowed to write a letter to him in prison. I hope they will treat him mercifully. I pray for him constantly."

It is not insignificant, therefore, that she should write a life of St. Catherine of Siena, the active contemplative on whose life Josephine modelled her own life in so many ways. "It requires more courage," she would say, "to be alone with God, than that needed to meet human opposition—the courage to cry, 'I will not let thee go, unless thou bless me'; and to have the egotism hunted out of one's soul."

A stained glass window in Liverpool Cathedral commemorates her life and work, and she is honored in the Church of England's Alternative Service Book as a social reformer, wife, and mother. The Church of England reluctantly decided to honor her in its revised calendar of saints (December 30) in 1980, when the motion was first defeated by four votes in the General Synod, only to be reinstated by a single vote in the House of Bishops

When the prolific painter G.F. Watts was invited to do his series of portraits for his Hall of Fame series of those who had "made the century," he asked Josephine Butler to "look into Eternity, looking at something no one else sees" while she sat for him. When Josephine saw the completed portrait she said that she felt inclined to burst into tears.

"I will tell you why....Your picture has brought back to me all that I suffered, and the sorrows through which the Angel of God's presence brought me out alive."

"God and one woman make a majority," she had once said, and her life and witness proved the truth of her statement.

Our Experience

Our sanctification and vocation belong together: our need is God's opportunity! We do not get well first and then in our strength and in our health seek some way in which God can use us in his service. Rather, we discover our health, salvation and sanctification in the doing of God's will: we become what God would have us be, by going where God would have us go. Josephine Butler recovered her sanity and attained to her sanctity in God's service, because she had an open wound of need in her bereavement and grief. Frederick Buechner reminds us that we generally find the good news all among the bad news. Josephine Butler found the good news of God's love for sinners among the "bad news" and darkness of her need and the open space left in her life and heart by the death of her little daughter. The whole of Josephine's vocation developed from that tragic bereavement. That does not mean that God caused the death of little Eva. Such an interpretation of tragedy would be totally incompatible with our knowledge of God as love in the face of Jesus Christ. Yet, with hindsight, we can often see (as Josephine herself eventually could) how God can use the "bad news" of Eva's death to draw Josephine out, to transform sadness into greater love, and transform the wounds of grief into the motivation for vocation and service.

Through her suffering, Josephine found herself always on the side of the oppressed, the downcast, the abused, and those who have no helper. Yet, none of this was born of a cool ideological persuasion, but rather from a passionate sympathy that can only come from a very close identification with all who suffer.

For so it was with God in Christ. Jesus comes to us where we are, and in his suffering identifies with sinners precisely because, thank God, we do not have a high priest "who is unable to sympathize with our weaknesses, but one who in every respect has been tempted as we are, yet without sin" (Heb. 4:15). Josephine Butler's work among and loving care for prostitutes and for the abused did not spring from a moralistic, self-righteous, condescending attitude. Rather, it sprang from a deep and heartfelt calling to go out of her own need among those in greater need, and so to find the love of God and the features of Christ in the needy, the outcast, and the unloved: in fact, in just those people and places where he promised us we could always find him. In so doing, it was in her vocation that Josephine found her sanity, her healing, and her salvation, for it really is in loving that we are loved, "in pardoning that we are pardoned, and in dying that we are born to eternal life."

WEEK FIVE: FRIDAY

And they went through the region of Phrygia and Galatia,
having been forbidden by the Holy Spirit to speak the
word in Asia. And when they had come opposite Mysia,
they attempted to go into Bithynia, but the Spirit of Jesus
did not allow them; so, passing by Mysia, they went
down to Troas. And a vision appeared to Paul in the
night: a man of Macedonia was standing beseeching him
and saying, "Come over to Macedonia and help us." And
when he had seen the vision, immediately we sought to
go on into Macedonia, concluding that God had called us
to preach the gospel to them. (Acts 16:6–10)

The Witness of Scripture

God's call belongs to a whole strategy of mission. However, it is usually possible to see this strategy only with
hindsight: seldom with foresight. In this second missionary
journey of St. Paul, Luke tells how Paul came to a real turning point in the geography of that missionary enterprise. Of
course, in Paul's day there was no line of demarcation between Asia and Europe, and any person sailing across the
Aegean Sea would not be conscious of traveling between
two continents at all. Rather, they would only be aware that
they were traveling from the eastern shores to the western
shores of the Aegean, which were at that time simply two
provinces within the one Roman Empire. However, in reality, when Paul and his party were called over by the man
from Macedonia, they were bringing into Europe Christianity and all that it would come to mean in the next two thousand years. Campbell Morgan[1] comments, "That invasion of
Europe was not in the mind of Paul, but it was evidently in
the mind of the Holy Spirit." John Stott[2] comments further,
"With the benefit of hindsight, knowing that Europe became
the first Christian continent and was, until fairly recently,

---

[1] Morgan, G. Campbell, *The Acts of the Apostles*, Fleming H. Revell 1924;
Pickering and Inglis, 1946, p. 287.
[2] John Stott, *The Spirit, the Church and the World*, I.V.P. 1990, p. 258.

the main base for missionary outreach to the rest of the world, we can see what an epoch-making development this was."

This becomes even more striking when you look more carefully at the geography of this passage. The most natural and reasonable thing for Paul and his companions to do was first to look southwest along the Via Sebaste to the coast—to Colosse and to Ephesus. In some mysterious way this way was blocked to them. Yet, if that was not to be the way, then surely they should turn north until they reached the border of Mysia, entering Bithynia, the province situated on the southern shore of the Black Sea, that included impressive and strategic cities such as Nicea and Nicomedia. But no—in some strange way "the Spirit of Jesus did not allow them."

The whole story reminds one a little of Balaam's ass in the Old Testament, and perhaps it should. For if we are to go where God sends us, then our vocation and calling will make an ass of all of us at some point. Our enterprise will appear foolishness to people, if it is to partake of the strategy and wisdom of God and to be anointed by the power of the Spirit. Our efforts need to belong to the larger plan, to the providence and strategy of a God who calls and sends, and who is the principal Messenger, as well as the message.

The Witness of the Saints

SAINT PATRICK (ca. 389–ca. 461)

"After a few years I was in Britain," wrote Patrick, "and there verily I saw in the night visions a man whose name was Victorious coming as it were from Ireland with countless letters. And he gave me one of them, and I read the beginning of the letter which was entitled, 'The voice of the Irish,' and while I was reading aloud the beginning of the letter, I thought that at that very moment I heard the voice of them who lived beside the wood of Foclut which is nigh unto the western sea. And this they cried, as with one mouth: 'We beseech thee, holy youth, to come and walk among us once more.'"

On the journey back to Ireland after his exile, Patrick and those who were with him were met by a group of clerics coming from Ireland with the news of the death of their bishop, Paladius. So it was that Patrick was chosen and consecrated bishop on his arrival in Ireland in 432, where he was to remain as apostle and evangelist until his death some thirty years later.

During his evangelizing crusades to Ireland, he met with much opposition from the Druids. "Patrick was supremely a man of prayer," wrote Lord Longford. "He saw visions and heard voices. His prayer was nourished on biblical imagery and biblical language."

Christ with me, Christ before me,
Christ behind me, Christ in me,
Christ under me, Christ over me,
Christ to right of me, Christ to left of me.
Christ in lying down, Christ in sitting, Christ in rising up.
Christ in the heart of every person who may think of me!
Christ in the mouth of every one who may speak of me!
Christ in every eye which may look on me!
Christ in every ear, which may hear me.

(St. Patrick's Breastplate)

St. Patrick's Breastplate is generally supposed to be the prayer which Patrick used to protect him spiritually, and in every way, against the Druids. However, nothing daunted the apostle of the Irish from organizing the scattered Christian communities and from extending the influence of the church. Legends abound about the life and work of Patrick. In 444, according to the Annals of Ulster, the cathedral church of Armagh, the primatial See of Ireland, was founded in Patrick's day and after a short time became the center of education as well as of ecclesiastical administration for the church in Ireland.

Patrick possibly died and was buried about the year 461, and tradition tells us that his body was laid to rest at Saul on Strangford Lough, where he had built one of his very first churches.

Our Experience

Since the dawn of time, God has been calling the most unlikely people to go to the most unpromising places with the most absurd and contradictory message.

"Come over to Macedonia," says the man in Paul's night vision. "Come and walk among us once more," says the voice of the Irish to Patrick in his exile and in his night visions. In both cases, the outcome was of strategic importance. In the former case, the word of the gospel entered Europe, and in the latter instance, the apostolic voice came to evangelize Ireland. In many ways Paul, could be forgiven for believing, as a Roman citizen, that Greece was the last place on earth in which he would ever be called to witness. Patrick could equally be forgiven for believing that Ireland, from which he had been exiled, would never bear fruit from his preaching, for after all, "a prophet is never without honor except in his own country." So never say "never" if you are seeking to respond to God's call.

Furthermore, part of the irony of vocation involves closed doors as well as open doors! It is significant that Paul recognizes an open door—incidentally, one of his favorite phrases—because so many doors seem to have closed for him. He was probably at the end of his tether, feeling downcast and finished, in the "night time" of his missionary enthusiasms. It is at such moments, when we are finished, that God can begin replacing our fixations with his real openings.

"God is working his purpose out as year succeeds to year," we sing in the great missionary hymn. For it is his prevenient grace that goes ahead to prepare a place for Christ himself to come. In the gospel missionary charge to the seventy, the geography of their missionary endeavors directs the seventy to those very places to which Jesus himself eventually intends to go. What other kind of missionary work would we possibly ever dare to undertake? Christ always goes ahead of us to prepare that place, and then, as part of a kind of divine joke, looks over his shoulder to see who should be called to "come over" to help him in *his* mission. For the Holy Spirit is the prime evangelist, and all our labors must be in companionship with him, who is always one step ahead of us.

So, humanly speaking, we must always retain a large element of humor in our sense of vocation. Whenever we look around at those whom God has called for some great work in his mission and ministry, he or she is nearly always the very *last* person we would ever have chosen: "God, you have to be joking, surely you did not really mean to call me, or did you?" Eusebius, the fourth-century historian, tells us with some authority that Paul was, humanly speaking, the last person in the world you would ever have expected to be called to be the great Apostle to the Gentiles: "a little man, a big red nose, bandy legs and not able to speak very well!" So it was with Moses and with all God's chosen people—including St. Patrick, who has always been a bit of a joke. So in his letter to the Corinthians, Paul remarks (and after all, he should know): "Consider your call, brethren; not many of you were wise according to worldly standards; not many were powerful, not many were of noble birth; but God chose what is foolish in the world to shame the wise, God chose what is weak in the world to shame the strong, God chose what is low and despised in the world, even things that are not, to bring to nothing things that are, so that no human being might boast in the presence of God" (1 Cor. 1:26–29).

WEEK FIVE: SATURDAY

And they put forward two, Joseph called Barsabbas, who was surnamed Justus, and Matthias. And they prayed and said, "Lord, who knowest the hearts of all men, show which one of these two thou hast chosen to take the place in this ministry and apostleship from which Judas turned aside, to go to his own place." And they cast lots for them, and the lot fell on Matthias; and he was enrolled with the eleven apostles. (Acts 1:23–26)

The Witness of Scripture

God's call comes through a church guided by Scripture and earnest in prayer, and which has the kind of "common sense" that could be the product only of the Holy Spirit.

Scripture led them to see the need to fill the place of Judas; Peter stood up and referred to the Scriptures (Acts 1:20). Common sense then took over and, informed by the Holy Spirit, told the apostles that whoever replaced Judas must have the same qualifications as Judas and the rest of the Twelve. These qualifications would include the need for him to have been with the larger band of disciples "all the time that the Lord Jesus went in and out among us." "Beginning from the baptism of John until the day when he [Jesus] was taken up from them." And then, finally, they turned to earnest prayer—to Jesus, whose call had been so formative in their own vocation back in the old days of Galilee.

Then by drawing lots, and leaving sufficient room for the hand of the Lord to show the apostles the person that Jesus had already chosen, the "election" was complete.

For, although the call may well come *through* the church, nevertheless it is always the call of Jesus, as Lord of his church.

One can even question whether or not the apostles got it right. One reputable biblical commentator suggests that the Twelve, in fact, got this wrong. "The election of Matthias was wrong," wrote Campbell Morgan.[3] "He was a good man, but the wrong man for this position....I am not prepared to omit Paul from the Twelve, believing that he was God's man for the filling of the gap."

In a sense, we might well ask whether it matters at all. The church does not have to be infallible, even if it could be! It merely has to be faithful and to allow Jesus to be Lord of his church. Then, and only then, can God override all our wrong decisions in his way and in his time.

---

[3] Morgan, G. Campbell, *The Acts of the Apostles*, Fleming H. Revell 1924; Pickering and Inglis, 1946, pp. 19-20.

The Witness of the Saints

SAINT AMBROSE (ca. 339–397)

Tradition says that it all started when a child cried out, "Ambrosius for bishop! Ambrosius for bishop!" As proconsul and governor of the provinces of Liguria and Aemilia in Italy, Ambrose presided at the election of a new bishop for Milan on the death of the Arian bishop, Auxentius, in 374. The election was foreseen as a bitter party struggle between the Arians and the Catholics. Each wanted its own candidate. While Ambrose was addressing the people on the need for an orderly election, the child cried out. Both parties took up the cry to the astonishment of Ambrose who, though highly respected for his upright and forthright life as a political leader, was not yet even baptized. In spite of the protestations of Ambrose to the contrary, the decision was taken as a unanimous call from the church for the proconsul to become bishop. The call of God had been expressed through the voice of the church—even the voice of a child.

So, only eight days after his ensuing baptism, Ambrose was consecrated bishop of Milan on December 7, 374. By training he had been a lawyer. Now he had to be a teacher of the Christian faith and resist in the name of the gospel all attempts to pervert Christian doctrine (especially those of the Arians), and to refuse to permit the attitudes of the prevailing culture to call the tune. In all of this, Ambrose proved to be an exemplary bishop. He taught the Scriptures daily in his cathedral. He studied the Scriptures daily for long hours in his study. St. Augustine gives us a close and detailed picture of Bishop Ambrose sitting in his house during the brief intervals between incessant business with his eyes fixed on the Bible and its accompanying commentaries, oblivious of everything else that was going on around him. Indeed, for Augustine, Ambrose as the teaching bishop was an essential link in the chain of events that eventually led the greatest African bishop—Augustine—to faith in Jesus Christ.

Throughout his episcopal ministry, Ambrose was always bold in withstanding Arianism which had become the religion of the court, which was located in Milan. Ambrose supported the full catholic doctrine of the person of Christ in the face of great political as well as theological opposition. He proved to be a strong and just bishop in a time of great upheavals in church and state, and indeed, to be a model bishop for successive ages, as an outstanding ecclesiastical statesman, preacher, teacher, pastor, and man of God.

Our Experience

God's calling can and frequently does come to us through the church—a church which should be open to the prompting of the Holy Spirit. After all, that was the way that Matthias was called to fill the place of Judas. That was the way (the very unexpected way) that Ambrose was called to be an apostle and bishop of Milan. It is very much the way the pope of Rome is called to this day.

Yet, notice that it is not a method that seeks to copy the parliamentary procedures of democracy, and note how the church falls into disrepute and fragmentation when it models its decision making upon the world's methods. That is how parties and factions arise in the church, as we play with majorities, with winners and losers, in a process which reflects the best the world can manage. Christians have access to a much better way.

It is consensus through the communion of the Holy Spirit which should form the mind of the church. Many parishes in renewal are adopting this method of decision making in their congregations and, far from finding it a slower and less efficient method, they are finding the very opposite: it is proving to be a remarkably efficient, effective, and smooth method for discerning the will of God and his call to his people. The church in Jerusalem, after prayer in the Spirit, came to a consensus on the potentially highly divisive matter of Gentile conversion and chose Paul and Barnabas for special apostolic work to the Gentiles.

All God's people are called to ministry by their baptism. Yet, there are diversities of ministry and spiritual gifts, for "God has appointed in the church first apostles, second prophets, third teachers, then workers of miracles, then healers, helpers, administrators, speakers in various kinds of tongues" (1 Cor. 12:28). Another list in the New Testament includes "evangelists" and "pastors," yet all are for one purpose, namely, "to equip the saints for the work of ministry, for building up the body of Christ, until we all attain to the unity of the faith and of the knowledge of the Son of God, to mature manhood, to the measure of the stature of the fullness of Christ" (Eph. 4:12-13).

So we are all called by our baptism to that one ministry with differing gifts, and all members of the Body of Christ are men and women who have a vocation. Sometimes—in fact, more often than not—it is helpful to involve the local congregation in discerning those gifts and in calling out of particular people for particular ministries, training, appointing, anointing, and commissioning them to be sent out to do God's will in his Church, as his Church, and for his world.

Offering, Obedience and Life for Others

Then I said, "Here am I! Send me."

INTRODUCING WEEK SIX

To live for others, as opposed to each person for him- or herself, is the new dynamic introduced by Jesus into the evolution of our humanity. Since the dawn of time, as far as we can see, the law of the jungle; the survival of the fittest and every man for himself have brought our world many times to the very brink of disaster and self-destruction.

"Greater love has no man than this, that a man lay down his life for his friends" (John 15:13). Jesus comes to introduce the virus of new, priestly life (life for others) into the body of our humanity. The "greater love" is that love embodied in a life lived for others. Furthermore, it is the priestly life of intercession—the willingness to go before the judge on someone else's behalf. Even more, it is the willingness to stand in their very shoes and take, on their behalf, the very worst that others can do to us.

So Jesus is both priest and victim as, to a lesser extent, Maximilian Kolbe was also himself both priest and victim. He stood in for someone else, as St. Alban many years before had also stood in for somebody else. It's catching on— this life for others! Jesus the Christ stood in for Jesus Barabbas on Good Friday. It is not fair, of course—Barabbas did not get what he deserved. He did not, but then, thank God, neither do we!

This laying down of our lives for others and this self-emptying offering of ourselves in worship are the essential chemistry of life in the kingdom. It means, of course, the

death of the old ego, in order that what is at work *in* us, is at
work essentially *through* us. It is God's life and God's love,
channeled *through* us, that can flow into the world with its
needs and its disasters. Channels of his grace and his new
life—this is what the church should want and pray for most
earnestly. Channels of his grace and new life are what the
world needs also. All this is summarized in the powerful
words of the priest who offers this prayer on behalf of all
God's priestly people in the old Book of Common Prayer for
the Church of England:

> And here we offer and present unto thee, O Lord, our
> selves, our souls and bodies, to be a reasonable, holy, and
> living sacrifice unto thee....And although we be unworthy,
> through our manifold sins, to offer unto thee any sacri-
> fice, yet we beseech thee to accept this our bounden duty
> and service: not weighing our merits, but pardoning our
> offenses; through Jesus Christ our Lord. Amen.

Questions for Personal Reflection or Discussion in Groups

1. In what ways are there complementary characteristics between the sacrifice of motherhood and the sacrifice of
   priesthood?

2. Why are we so afraid to use our bodies in worship, and in
   what ways can we help people to express worship through
   their bodies?

3. What is the relationship between the ordained priesthood
   and the priesthood of all believers?

4. What is the next "roadblock" in my life that must go in
   order that I may more fully surrender myself to the Divine
   Will?

WEEK SIX: MONDAY

> On the third day, when Esther ended her prayer, she took
> off the garment in which she had worshipped, and ar-
> rayed herself in splendid attire. Then, majestically

adorned, after invoking the aid of the all-seeing God and Savior, she took her two maids with her, leaning daintily on one, while the other followed carrying her train....When she had gone through all the doors, she stood before the king. He was seated on his royal throne, clothed in the full array of his majesty, all covered with gold and precious stones. And he was most terrifying.

Lifting his face, flushed with splendor, he look at her in fierce anger. And the queen faltered, and turned pale and faint, and collapsed upon the head of the maid who went before her. Then God changed the spirit of the king to gentleness, and in alarm he sprang from his throne and took her in his arms until she came to herself. And he comforted her with soothing words, and said to her, "What is it, Esther? I am your brother. Take courage; you shall not die, for our law applies only to the people. Come near."

Then he raised the golden sceptre and touched it to her neck; and he embraced her, and said, "Speak to me."

(Esther 15:1-12, Apocryphal version)

The Witness of Scripture

Biblical commentators are deeply divided about the nature of the book of Esther. Few would rank it as literal and historical material, and most seem to prefer to speak of it as an "historical novel"—that is, a story rooted in the facts of history.

In any event, it is a good story. We can read it as an account of the brave witness by the Jewish queen, Esther, and her care for her people, who were under the pressure and tyranny of an alien culture. At great potential cost to herself, Queen Esther decides to go, unheralded, before the king to plead for her people, the Jewish exiles. (Her heroism lies in the fact that she could have received the death penalty, since the king had not summoned her into his presence.)

So the story grows with the telling! She passes through the various doors that divide the throne room from the rest of the palace, as she draws closer and closer to the royal presence.

God changes the spirit of the king to gentleness and the king, far from rejecting or condemning her, springs from his throne to greet her and offers the touch of the royal scepter to indicate that she is free to address the king on behalf of her people. In picture form, we see the work of intercession and of the royal priesthood at its clearest. Esther is not pleading her own cause, but she is pleading the cause of her people, and as such is acting as a priestly intercessor. She is offering her life for others and, as we know from the rest of the story, her intercession was granted.

The Witness of the Saints

SAINT MONICA (ca. 331–387)

"My son, as for myself, I now find no pleasure in this life," said Monica to her son Augustine as she lay dying in Ostia on their way home to North Africa in 387. "What I have still to do here and why I am here, I do not know. My hope in this world is already fulfilled. The one reason why I wanted to stay longer in this life was my desire to see you a catholic Christian before I die. My God has granted this in a way more than I had hoped. For I see you despising this world's success to become his servant. What more have I to do here?"

So, "on the ninth day of her illness," St. Augustine later tells us in his *Confessions*, "when she was aged fifty-six, and I was thirty-three, this religious and devout soul was released from the body."

Monica had been a devout Christian from her youth. She had married Patricius, a man of dissolute habits and a somewhat violent temper. They had three children, Navigius, Perpetua, and Augustine, who was the eldest. Although Monica had enrolled Augustine as a catechumen, when he would have been signed with the sign of the cross "and seasoned with salt"—that is salt would have been placed on the tongue as an act of exorcism—nevertheless he was not baptized as a child. The ministry and life of Monica as a mother of three children was supremely that of an intercessor. She had prayed for her husband, and now she prayed for her children, but especially for Augustine, the eldest and the brightest. However, until he was in his thirties, Augustine's life lacked direction, purpose, and faith. Monica was so distraught by Augustine's behavior that she had at one time pleaded with one of the bishops to exert influence upon her wayward son. She pressed the bishop with floods of tears, begging him to speak to Augustine about his soul. Not a little vexed, the bishop is reported to have said, "Go away from me; as you live, it cannot be that the son of these tears should perish."

And so when Augustine was dramatically converted in a garden in Milan in 386, the first person he rushed to tell was, naturally, Monica his mother, who was in the house. She was privileged to be with him for his baptism on Easter Eve the following year when he was baptized by Bishop Ambrose. Then on the return journey to Africa from Milan via the port of Rome, Ostia, where they were waiting for a ship to take the family party back to Algeria in Africa, there, Monica contracted a fever and died.

Her life's work was complete.

Our Experience

Intercession is not only a method of prayer, it is also a whole way of life—essentially the priestly life, life for others. In the Roman judiciary courts, the intercessor or advocate was the one who went before the judge on someone else's behalf to plead their cause. In the Old Testament, the story of Queen Esther is the story of priestly intercession. Queen Esther, at the risk of her life, went before the king to intercede for her people as surely as Monica went daily before the king of heaven to intercede for Augustine her son.

Such costly and sacrificial prayer springs from a whole attitude about life—life for others. The intercessor and priestly person is someone who *prays* for others, because he or she has first learned what it is to *live* for others. Furthermore, intercession is the essential quality of priestly life of which Aaron and his tribe are the prototypes in the Old Testament. The priests of Aaron would enter the Holy of Holies, bearing the names of the other tribes on the ephod over their heart, to plead for them before the throne of God.

Jesus in the New Testament is the unique high priest, but notice that he is also the victim. He shares in that greater love of the kingdom in which he "lays down his life for his friends." So love, life, and intercession in the New Testament are to the point of death. Jesus is the ultimate, perfect, sacrificial victim—life lived for others to the point of being ready to die for others. As such he is the one true high priest of our calling.

Monica had lived her life in just that way for Augustine, so that eventually Augustine might obtain real life through the life laid down by his mother. Her life and her prayer were one, as she is both mother and priestly intercessor for her son. Not surprisingly, once that prayer was answered and granted, there was no further point to life for Monica, and so she died, there in Ostia in her son's arms, now that he was securely in the arms of that other mother's Son, Jesus Christ.

Mothers make perhaps the most powerful intercessors for their sons. After all, the son comes to life within the mother, who in childbirth sheds her blood for him. Her heartbeat can itself be a prayer for the child within her.

It is significant that in many parishes it is the women—the old women, generally—who are the great army of intercessors. This is a ministry which can become more, not less, powerful with old age. It is often most effective among the housebound, widows, or people who are handicapped in other ways—in fact, among all those who "cannot do what they used to be able to do." It is through the ministry of intercession, as members of the priesthood of all believers, that they can and should exercise this most powerful and life-changing ministry of intercession. "Holy Monica, pray for us," that we, in turn, may pray for others before the throne of grace.

WEEK SIX: TUESDAY

And while he was at Bethany in the house of Simon the leper, as he sat at table, a woman came with an alabaster flask of ointment of pure nard, very costly, and she broke the flask and poured it over his head. But there were some who said to themselves indignantly, "Why was the ointment thus wasted? For this ointment might have been sold for more than three hundred denarii, and given to the poor." And they reproached her. But Jesus said, "Let her alone; why do you trouble her? She has done a beautiful thing to me. For you always have the poor with you, and whenever you will, you can do good to them; but you will not always have me. She has done what she could; she has anointed my body beforehand for burying. And truly, I say to you, wherever the gospel is preached in the whole world, what she has done will be told in memory of her." (Mark 14:3–9)

The Witness of Scripture

Mark places this gospel story at Bethany just outside Jerusalem and in the setting of Holy Week. He sees it as very closely related to the passion, suffering, and death of Christ. Luke, on the other hand, places a very similar story much earlier in his gospel. Mark does not say so but, nevertheless, the implication is that it was not the Pharisees on this occasion who objected to the "waste" of such precious ointment. Rather, for Mark, the objections arose from among the friends of Jesus. John puts the words of objection in the mouth of Judas and adds that Judas was a thief. John would have us realize that Judas would not have given the money raised from the sale of the ointment to the poor, but that he would have simply put it in his own pocket!

Be this all as it may, from whatever version we are reading, the lesson comes across loud and clear. Here is a totality of offering, oblation, and worship paid to the ultimate person—to God himself. This woman, whoever she was and when or wherever this event happened, has shown to the world a lesson of eternal significance so that "wherever the gospel is preached" this story will be told. God is worthy of the most costly worship and of our ultimate self-oblation. Like the story of the widow's mite, this woman also has given her all—her best.

It is interesting that throughout the history of the church, many lukewarm Christians feel uncomfortable when worship becomes excessive. They generally have a name for it. They call it "high church" or, more often today, "charismatic." Whenever the body and the senses become involved in worship, many people begin to talk among themselves indignantly, and begin to feel uncomfortable. So Luke tells us, for example, that she even let her hair down to wipe the feet of Jesus. This would signify, in the New Testament world of Palestine, that she was indeed a woman of the street and a woman of doubtful reputation. Yet, it takes this woman to teach the church the full-blooded, sacrificial, no-holds-barred worship of Jesus. Furthermore, Jesus accepts the ministry of anointing from this woman—and a woman of doubtful reputation, at that.

What does all this say to us about our worship and our lukewarm discipleship?

The Witness of the Saints

SAINT CLARE (ca. 1194–1253)

When Clare was just eighteen years old, St. Francis came to preach a Lent course of sermons at the church of San Giorgio in Assisi. The preaching of Francis touched the life of Clare in a deep and lasting way. On Palm Sunday that same year, she attended the cathedral in Assisi for the ceremony of the blessing of the palms by the bishop. When everyone else went forward to receive their olive branch from the bishop, Clare was seized with a sense of reticence and shyness and she remained in her place. The bishop noticed her and went straight down from the altar to give her the branch of palm. That evening, she ran away from home to the little town of Portiuncula, a mile or so away from Assisi, where St. Francis lived with his community. He and his brothers met Clare at the entrance to the chapel of our Lady of the Angels, lighted torches in hand. Before the altar in that chapel she laid aside her fine clothes (for she was from a wealthy and distinguished family). Francis cut her hair and gave her his penitential habit, which was the simplest of sackcloth tunics, tied at the waist with a cord. As there was no nunnery attached to the Order of Francis, at this time, Clare was temporarily placed in the Benedictine convent of St. Paul near Bastia.

It was not long before Clare was joined by friends and relatives. In 1215, Francis placed Clare as abbess, together with her sisters (the "Poor Clares" as they have come to be known), in a house close to the church of San Damiano on the outskirts of Assisi.

It was Sister Clare and the Poor Clares, more than the brothers of St. Francis, who really kept the rule of total poverty and simplicity in the spirit of St. Francis.

Several daughter houses were soon founded in Italy, France, and Germany, with an austere rule which went beyond any that women had previously undertaken. It was only after great determination and many struggles that Clare obtained for her sisters at Assisi, Perugia, and Florence the *privilegium paupertatis* from Pope Gregory IX that allowed them to maintain their original state of total poverty.

Our Experience

Self-offering, self-emptying, and worship are the point of all life. To the penitent prostitute at Bethany is given the privilege of anointing the Anointed One. In doing this, she shows to us the essence of true worship—total self-abandonment to the divine providence of love. She offers herself to Jesus—herself, her "soul and body, to be a reasonable, holy and living sacrifice." She knows in her bones the secret of the cross—namely, that life freely given away is life kept for ever, while, paradoxically, life that is hoarded and kept for self is eventually lost for ever.

In a word, she has discovered that life for others is the secret of all life worthy of the name. Clare and her sisters who surrendered everything are truly enriched, so that they have something of eternal value to give to the poor—namely, love. You cannot do that until you have learned the costly power of worship and self-oblation, and then, in doing it, you will not only be giving to the poor, but also giving to God—for "as much as you have done it to the least of one of these my brethren, you have done it to me," says the Lord.

So perhaps Mother Teresa of Calcutta stands as the most powerful sign of contradiction to our world—a world which grasps at power and riches. Power becomes authority when it is given away. Something is much more precious and valuable when it is a gift than when it is something which we have earned. So Mother Teresa turns all our world of values upside down. She has possibly had the most powerful effect upon people (especially young people) of anyone in this generation.

Yet, the worship of God and the service of the poor are not two opposites. Rather, they converge in the person of Jesus. Our adoration before the Blessed Sacrament—the Body of Christ—and our love and care for Christ's poor (also the Body of Christ *in* the poor) are worship and service, and in Christ they are inextricably bound together. The woman with the alabaster flask at Bethany is caring for and attending to the physical Body of the poor Christ with love and adoration. Mother Teresa in Calcutta cares for the mystical Body of Christ's poor with the same love and adoration. Both are examples of worship, and both are examples of service, for "when the worship is ended the service begins"! Both at Bethany and in Calcutta we see love, sacrificial self-giving, and a self-emptying of all to enable the free passage of the "greater love" into our impoverished world.

St. Clare loved beautiful things, but she learned to love beauty in things and in people much more because she had first found beauty in the face of Jesus. So, too, with the woman at Bethany. All her life, she had looked for that beauty in the bodily forms of God's creatures. At last, she found it in the face of her Creator, so how could she possibly now withhold anything? Now she would not only offer her body for his Body; now she would offer all that she had and all that she was. Such is the nature of "worship" and "reasonable service."

> Were the whole realm of nature mine,
> That were an offering far too small.
> Love so amazing, so Divine,
> Demands my soul, my life, my all.
>   (Isaac Watts)

WEEK SIX: WEDNESDAY

And on the first day of Unleavened Bread, when they sacrificed the passover lamb, his disciples said to him, "Where will you have us go and prepare for you to eat the

passover?" And he sent two of his disciples, and said to
them, "Go into the city, and a man carrying a jar of water
will meet you; follow him, and wherever he enters, say to
the householder, 'The teacher says, Where is my guest
room, where I am to eat the passover with my disciples?'
And he will show you a large upper room furnished and
ready; there prepare for us." And the disciples set out and
went to the city, and found it as he had told them; and
they prepared the passover. (Mark 14:12–16)

The Witness of Scripture

"Where on earth will Jesus eat the Passover?" Perhaps
that's what they all were asking. After all, "foxes have holes,
and birds of the air have nests, but the Son of man has nowhere to lay his head" (Matt. 8:20). It had always been like
that from the beginning. The inn back in Bethlehem was full
to capacity and there was no room for Jesus. They simply
laid him in a manger!

Has there ever really been room in our lives for Jesus?
Have we always offered him the small change of our lives?
The story of the good man of the house and the woman in
the house of Simon at Bethany are two glorious exceptions. They form part of the flare path for Christian discipleship and show us the way to the worship that leads to
heaven.

Frankly, this good man of the house sticks out like a sore
thumb! He is a real sign of contradiction. Certainly, "a man
carrying a jar of water" would have been a sign of contradiction in Jerusalem. Carrying water was the work of women
in the ancient world. Jesus tells his disciples to say that the
Master is requesting the use of the guest room; in Greek, it
was, in fact, the smallest room in the house. Yet, Jesus is con-
fident that this anonymous laymen, being who he was,
would offer not the guest room, but the best room—"the
large upper room, well-furnished."

The church is a gift from start to finish, because all life in
the kingdom is a gift. Generous, costly worship is the secret
that unlocks the doors to that kingdom, and in this passage,
we see Jesus and his disciples observing both their last Passover meal together and the first eucharist of history, as the

old way of the Law with its cautious limitations ushers in the new way of grace and generosity.

The Witness of the Saints

SAINT GREGORY THE GREAT (ca. 540–604)

Pope Gregory I—"the consul of God"—rightly called "the Great," was the first pope to have been a monk—a Benedictine; and throughout all his life, he was an ardent promoter of Benedictine monasticism.

In a country torn by war and civil strife, Rome suffered perhaps more than any other part of Italy in Gregory's time. Sacked four times in just over one century and conquered four times in twenty years, it was a city in ruins from pillage, fire, and earthquake.

Gregory was from a devout Roman patrician family. They had already produced two popes, and Gregory's mother, Silvia, was to be listed in the Roman list of saints after her death. Gregory received the best possible education of his day, and at the age of thirty, as one of the richest men in Rome, he rose to the highest civil office in the great city, that of prefect of Rome.

Suddenly, however, Gregory, like many of the finer men of those times, gave up everything for Christ. He sold his vast properties, giving the proceeds to the relief of the poor and to the founding of seven monasteries, six in Sicily and one (St. Andrew's) in Rome, which he himself entered at the age of thirty-four, and where he eventually became the abbot.

In 589, a severe plague broke out in Rome, and in January the following year, Pope Pelagius died of the disease. Gregory was unanimously chosen pope against his expressed will. His pontificate is distinguished for many reasons.

In the first place, he brought about peace with the warring Lombards. He wrote a definitive book on the work and office of a bishop *(Regula Pastoralis)*. The book was immensely formative for several centuries and was translated into several languages, and it shaped episcopacy in Europe for many centuries to come. He is responsible (through Augustine of Canterbury) for the special mission to the English in 597. His prolific sermons, writings, and letters were influential long after his death. He was a liturgist of some distinction, establishing and promoting in his *schola cantorum* the Gregorian chant and the singing of the liturgy which had to be of the best possible rendering.

Furthermore, he defended the rights, privileges, and responsibilities of the See of Rome against the opposing claims of Constantinople in the East, while he still adopted the modest title for himself of *servus servorum dei*—servant of the servants of God. "Almost his last action was to send a warm winter cloak to a poor bishop who suffered from the cold" (Butler).

Buried in St. Peter's in Rome and canonized by popular acclaim immediately after his death in 604, the epitaph on his tomb read, "After having conformed all his actions to his doctrines, the great consul of God went to enjoy eternal triumphs."

Our Experience

When the anonymous "good man of the house" of the gospel freely and willingly offers to Jesus not simply his "guest room," but rather his best room; not his smallest room, but that largest room "well furnished"; and not the room downstairs, but rather the room upstairs, we catch a glimpse of gospel gratitude that is at the very heart of Christian witness and worship. That good man of the house had learned to live eucharistically long before the eucharist was first celebrated in his upper room—the room which was destined to become the cenacle of the great catholic church of Jesus Christ.

He offered the best to Jesus, because for him it was clearly a case of nothing less than the best for God. Love goes out of its way; it always has. Perhaps Jesus had healed a member of that good man's family. In any event, Jesus could be sure that although he only requested the smallest guest room of the house, the man would offer his best room. He, the householder, would be displaced and go downstairs to observe the family Passover. Like David in the Old Testament, it was a case of refusing to "offer to the Lord that which" costs nothing. There was nothing cheap or half-hearted about that anonymous layman's offering, and there was everything that was cheerful about it.

George Herbert speaks of offering to God the "cream of all my heart." The composer Bach used to put the initials *AMDG* at the top of all his musical compositions: Latin for "to the greater glory of God." So, too, with Gregory the Great. He offered to the Lord all his political and administrative skills and the best of all he was or had—and all to the greater glory of God as a bishop in his church. It is not insignificant that Gregory should have been concerned about music of the best kind to be employed in the worship of the church. It is in the generosity of a grateful heart that the eucharist begins to work its transforming power. Gratitude to God for all that he has done and all that he is has moved people of wealth and artistic skills to delight in offering the best for the worship, glory, and service of God in beautiful buildings, art, design, vestments, and music. Wherever the gospel is truly preached and ministered, there will always be those who want to give to the church of their best as a "thank-offering" to the glory of God.

Gratitude from a generous heart is the raw material—the bread—of the eucharist. Gregory was essentially a big-hearted man, who in turn became a great apostle, leaving a stamp of excellence upon apostolic ministry which has glorified God in his church throughout the ages.

So the message of worship is the same to rich and poor alike; to the simple and to the clever; to the plain and to the attractive; to the brilliant and to the not so brilliant. For there is no room in that "upper room" of excellence and gratitude for envy, or jealousy, or small-mindedness. All alike are called to give all that they have in gratitude and generosity as a sacrificial, eucharistic, thank-offering for all that they have been given and continue to receive from the Lord. All the great miracles occur in the environment of that large upper room of a grateful heart: eucharist, washing of feet, resurrection, healing, and possibly even in that same upper room, the power of Pentecost—all that is possible in the context of gratitude and *largesse du coeur*. That is the only trouble with this Jesus: once he gets a foot into the door of your heart there is a serious danger that he will take over! After all, he only came for dinner, and just look where it all ended up!

> What shall I give Him, poor as I am?
> If I were a shepherd, I would bring a lamb.
> If I were a wise man, I would do my part:
> Yet what shall I give Him? Give Him my heart.
> (Christina Rossetti)

WEEK SIX: THURSDAY

And taking with him Peter and the two sons of Zebedee, he began to be sorrowful and troubled. Then he said to them, "My soul is very sorrowful, even to death; remain here, and watch with me." And going a little farther he fell on his face and prayed, "My Father, if it be possible, let this cup pass from me; nevertheless, not as I will, but as thou wilt." And he came to the disciples and found them sleeping; and he said to Peter, "So, could you not watch with me one hour? Watch and pray that you may not enter into temptation; the spirit indeed is willing, but the flesh is weak." Again, for the second time, he went away and prayed, "My Father, if this cannot pass unless I drink it, thy will be done." And again he came and found them sleeping, for their eyes were heavy. So, leaving them again, he went away and prayed for the third time, saying the same words. Then he came to the disciples and said to them, "Are you still sleeping and taking your rest? Behold, the hour is at hand, and the Son of man is betrayed into the hands of sinners. Rise, let us be going; see, my betrayer is at hand." (Matthew 26:37–46)

The Witness of Scripture

The most important thing to note about the story of the passion of Christ in the garden of Gethsemane involves knowing just when and where all this took place.

In the first place, Christ's passion coincided exactly with the Passover. On that night in Gethsemane, the bright Passover moon would be at its fullest, shining brightly in the sky over the Mount of Olives and over the city of Jerusalem just below. You could have read a newspaper in the moonlight

on that strange Passover night. That was *when* it happened.
Now add to that picture the circumstances in which it happened. The garden of Gethsemane rests on the side of the
Mount of Olives, overlooking the old city of Jerusalem, which
is in fact only a matter of yards away from that garden where
Jesus was kneeling in prayer.

Can you see now how Jesus was not taken by surprise
or off his guard when he was arrested in the garden? He
would have been able to see the temple guard coming for
him. In other words, he was free to escape, right up to the
very last moment. But the poignant reality of this story is
even more astonishing. He could have escaped so easily, yet
he chose not to. He was free to withhold this final offering
to the Father, yet he was also totally free to make the ultimate offering for sin. He freely chose to go all the way and
totally out of his way for the love of you and me. We might
well ask, how far we are prepared to go out of our way for
him who went all the way for us?

"Only Jesus was free not to sin" (Augustine). Many of our
sins, as well as our virtues, are in fact Hobson's choices. Even
our virtues often belong to compulsive patterns of behavior.
We are often driven even when we are doing good deeds, let
alone when we are doing sinful ones. Yet, Jesus is not driven
at all. He is in the driving seat from start to finish, freely offering himself as a sacrifice for the sins of the whole world.

There is something awesome about this degree of freedom. It is a mystery, but it is a mystery in which the saints
have a small part to play.

The Witness of the Saints

SAINT POLYCARP, BISHOP OF SMYRNA (ca. 69–ca. 155)

"Fourscore and six years have I served Him and He hath
done me no wrong," said the ancient Bishop Polycarp as he
stood in the stadium before the proconsul and the angry
and ungodly crowd on February 23 in the year 155. The fourth-
century historian Eusebius tells us that, as the aged bishop
entered the stadium under arrest, "there came a voice to
him from heaven, 'Be strong, Polycarp, and play the man.'"

Polycarp was one of the most famous of the little group of early, first century bishops known as the Apostolic Fathers. He had been a disciple of St. John the Evangelist. He had kissed the chains of St. Ignatius of Antioch when he had passed through Smyrna, where Polycarp was the bishop, on his way to martyrdom. Now, at the age of eighty-six, Polycarp was to face death himself for the faith of Christ.

"Swear, and I will release you; curse Christ," shouted the proconsul.

"How can I blaspheme my King who saved me?" retorted Polycarp. "If you vainly imagine that I would 'swear by the genius of Caesar,' as you say...hear plainly that I am a Christian."

While the crowd roared for crude entertainment, the proconsul said, "I have wild beasts; if you will not change your mind, I will throw you to them."

"Bid them be brought," retorted Polycarp. "Change of mind from better to worse is not a change that we are allowed; but to change from wrong to right is good."

"If you despise the beasts, unless you change your mind, I shall have you burnt."

But Polycarp said, "You threaten the fire that burns for an hour, and after a little while is quenched; for you are ignorant of the fire of judgement to come and of everlasting punishment reserved for the ungodly. But why delay? Do what you wish."

At two o'clock on that February afternoon, as the flames consumed his body, Polycarp died praying to God.

Our Experience

The ultimate offering is the one great all-sufficient offering of Christ. He has freely given his life. We did not take it—rather, he willingly offered it. So if we are to follow him, it will have to be: "Take my life and let it be consecrated, Lord, to thee": easy to sing, but not so easy to do.

Yet, in every generation, some men and women have responded literally to that call, and, where and when necessary, they have counted not their lives as dear to themselves, but have been ready to lay down their lives for the love of the Crucified. However, we must not see martyrdom as an end in itself. We must not romanticize martyrdom: it is always a bloody mess. Suffering is not good in itself. It can become good only because of what God can do with it. God does not will our death. He wills only total union with himself, and the Bible is adamant from cover to cover: no one can see God face to face and live. Union with God demands that we pass *through* the door of death. The road home back to the glory of God inevitably passes *through* the darkness of the world and *through* the valley of the shadow of death. Yet, it was for "the joy that was set before Him" that Christ was given strength to "endure the cross, despising the shame," and all this so that eventually, on the other side of death, Jesus might be reunited with his Father and with ours— "seated at the right hand of the throne of God" (Heb. 12:2). Of course, it is only natural and indeed healthy that Jesus in his humanity and even more in his divinity longs for some other way to do the will of God and to return to his Father. He did not seek martyrdom or glorify death: nor must we. It is the last enemy, and it stands between us and total union with God in Christ.

Most of us do not have to choose between life in this world, where the best is communion with God, and the consummation of life after death, where we shall be offered perfect union with God in Christ. As a matter of fact, Paul said that he honestly could not make up his mind which of the two was the best for him at that stage. However, when he was given the chance to choose, tradition tells us that he chose the direct path home to God via the road of martyrdom. So did Polycarp, in his old age, as Jesus did in his youth. For sooner or later, either inevitably or by choice, we shall need to go bravely forward to meet him face to face, through the unknown and the dark valley. Jesus must be Lord of our death as well as of our life, and he must have the last word in this as in all other things. We must seek to glorify him in our death as in our life.

Whether or not it is by choice, to both alike, in youth as well as in old age, a special grace and gift is given. We do not know what is on the other side. We are ignorant of the geography, the furnishings, and fittings of life after death.

Yet one thing is sure. The One with whom we have been in communion in this life will be the same as the One in union with whom we shall go through the darkness of death to the light of the glory beyond. It is our friendship with the same Jesus, "yesterday, today and forever," which we have come to recognize and know this side of the grave, whom we shall see more fully in the life beyond. He is with us at every point of the journey, and constitutes the true continuity of our life beyond the grave. For "this is eternal life," to know God and him whom he sent (John 17:3). It is our relationship with God that is eternal and stronger than death: all else is mortal and ephemeral.

WEEK SIX: FRIDAY

> It was now about the sixth hour, and there was darkness over the whole land until the ninth hour, while the sun's light failed; and the curtain of the temple was torn in two. Then Jesus, crying with a loud voice, said, "Father, into thy hands I commit my spirit!" And having said this he breathed his last. (Luke 23:44–46)

The Witness of Scripture

It is Luke who gives us the first word from the cross, and it is Luke who gives us the last word from the cross. Both, alike, are directed to Jesus' Father and ours.

The first word from the cross is written by Luke deliberately in two parallel, imperfect tenses. "They crucified him... and he said, 'Father forgive...'" (Luke 23:33,34). Strictly this should more accurately be translated something along these lines: "As they were crucifying him, he kept on saying, 'Father forgive....'" As they were knocking in the nails, Jesus kept on saying, "Father, forgive."

It takes a long time to nail a man to a piece of wood. "How many times should my brother sin against me and I forgive him?" Peter had once asked. "Seven times?" Peter, of all people, should have known just how many times he would need to be forgiven—three times, at least, in the last twenty-four hours—so, what about a lifetime of reluctant discipleship? Thank God that the first word from the cross, then, was not just said once by Jesus, but repeated many times. I need to know that there is a whole credit balance of forgiveness on which I can draw infinitely. I need to hear many times the reassuring gospel words, "Go in peace, the Lord has put away all your sins."

So much for the first word from the cross.

What about the last word from the cross? Luke records this in the past historic tense. Jesus said, only once, "Father, into thy hands I commend my spirit." There can only be one "Amen," and Jesus is the only one who has said it once and for all—once upon a time, for all time. He is the "one perfect, and sufficient sacrifice, oblation, and satisfaction, for the sins of the whole world." Every other high priest has to make the offering many times, but he has made it once and for all—the perfect offering and act of obedience that is the only worship ultimately acceptable to the Father.

The Witness of the Saints

SAINT MAXIMILIAN KOLBE (1894–1941)

"Don't you see it as an honor to suffer? Just think, Jesus has chosen us to share his sufferings. Don't forget. He too was persecuted and rejected by all. He knew indescribable sadness and exhaustion. They beat him, nailed Him to the cross, ridiculed Him....But he forgave them, and so should we."

These are the words of Father Maximilian Kolbe, the Polish saint and martyr of our generation. As a little boy, he had received a vision of Mary holding two crowns, offering him a choice between a white and a red one. The white crown signified a life dedicated to purity and celibacy, while the red crown suggested a martyr's crown. The young boy chose both.

And so it was that as prisoner no. 16670 in Auschwitz, and also as a priest, he volunteered to die in the place of another prisoner who pleaded not to die because he was married with a wife and children. A prisoner had escaped, and now ten men would pay the price with their lives. "I am a Catholic priest and I want to die in his place. He has a wife and family," pleaded Maximilian in the courtyard as the ten men were being selected to die.

And so it was that nine men and one priest went to the specially constructed underground starvation bunker. Father Maximilian had at all times during his imprisonment at Auschwitz striven to help his comrades to win the ultimate victory, namely, to love and forgive his jailers. To the end, in that death bunker he ministered to his fellow men, until only four were left alive out of the ten. Because the cell was needed for other victims, Father Maximilian and the remaining three prisoners were given a lethal injection. Moments later, Father Maximilian died, "his head bowed, his serenely beautiful face radiant."

The next day, the body of the supposedly escaped prisoner was found, drowned in a latrine. Apparently, all a dreadful waste?

"This was victory won over all the system of contempt and hate in man and what was divine in man, victory like that won by our Lord Jesus Christ on Calvary," said Pope John Paul II at the canonization of Maximilian Mary Kolbe in Rome on October 10, 1982. In St. Peter's Square in Rome on that day, there were 150,000 people, including Francis Gajowniczek, the man whose place Father Maximilian had voluntarily taken. With that man were his wife, his children, and his children's children.

Our Experience

In an age of competitive individualism, when it's every man for himself and a question of the survival of the fittest, the priestly life of intercession and celibacy and the challenge of life for others stand out as curious signs of contradiction. For if, in the kingdoms of this world, it is every man for himself, we need to know that in the kingdom of God it will always be essentially "people for others," and that is what is meant by living the life of the priesthood of all believers. The ordained priesthood, married or celibate, is God's gift to his church to ensure that the life of the church is essentially priestly. Yet, at the same time, the church is intended to be God's gift to the world to ensure that one day the whole universe will catch this new way of life—the priestly life of "man for others." For the many are saved by the few, as surely as the few are saved by the One.

So it was that Jesus taught his disciples the ultimate lesson about this kind of life on the evening before he laid down his life for others. "Greater love has no man than this, that a man lays down his life for his friends" (John 15:13). But that is not just a way to die. We have taken the bite out of those revolutionary words by placing them on the stone epitaphs of the dead when Christ intended them to be inscribed in our hearts as the new way of life. After speaking about this yet more excellent way of life, Jesus went ahead and demonstrated it when he washed the feet of the disciples and then set his feet on the last stage of the journey to Calvary. It's not fair, of course. At three o'clock on that Good Friday afternoon, while Jesus Barabbas is having drinks all around in the local bar, the other Jesus (not in his place, but certainly on his behalf) is sweating it out on Calvary. "But don't think you've got off scot free, Jesus Barabbas: your turn will come!"

For Maximilian Kolbe, it was not simply a question of dying as a priest in the place of someone else. Rather, it was because he had always lived that way that eventually he was able to die that way. In the food lines at Auschwitz, he was forever giving up his place for somebody else.

"The church," said Archbishop William Temple, "is the only society which exists for the sake of those who are not members of it." We do not go to church in order to save our own miserable little souls. That has already been done for us. We always go (or should always go) on behalf of others who do not go. We should go before the Lord on behalf of others to make intercession for them, as Christ our great high priest has ascended into heaven and ever lives to intercede for us on earth. In that way, the Christian is baptized and, literally, marked for life in order to represent Jesus Christ for others. That is the new life and the new way of life in the kingdom. St. Alban did it when he stood in the line of martyrdom on somebody else's behalf. St. Maximilian did it and millions of other intercessory, priestly people have done it—and all because Jesus has done it, once and for all.

Of course, all this goes against the grain of everything we were ever brought up in this world to believe or to do. It goes against the grain of everything the kingdoms of this world would teach us, yet it is supremely the most positive and creative sign of contradiction in human history, bringing us back again and again from the edge of that precipice of self-destruction. Yet, this sign is essentially cruciform in shape and is most powerful in its capacity to turn this universe around. It is the only way forward for the history of the world, and in every generation there have to be the "few" who are ready to stand in for the "many." When history is finally retold in the light of total knowledge, it will be the few who will be seen to have made all the difference in the world, because of the One and on behalf of the many. "Holy Maximilian, pray for us."

WEEK SIX: SATURDAY

And from Miletus he sent to Ephesus and called to him the elders of the church. And when they came to him, he said to them:
"You yourselves know how I lived among you all the time from the first day that I set foot in Asia, serving the Lord with all humility and with tears and trials which befell me through the plots of the Jews; how I did not shrink from declaring to you anything that was profitable, and teaching you in public and from house to house, testifying both to Jews and to Greeks of repentance to God and of faith in our Lord Jesus Christ. And now, behold, I am going to Jerusalem, bound in the Spirit, not knowing what shall befall me there; except that the Holy Spirit testifies to me in every city that imprisonment and afflictions await me. But I do not account my life of any value nor as precious to myself, if only I may accomplish my course and the ministry which I received from the Lord Jesus, to testify to the gospel of the grace of God. And now, behold, I know that all you among whom I have gone preaching the kingdom will see my face no more...."
And when he had spoken thus, he knelt down and

prayed with them all. And they all wept and embraced
Paul and kissed him, sorrowing most of all because of the
word he had spoken, that they should see his face no more.
And they brought him to the ship. (Acts 20:17–25, 36–38)

The Witness of Scripture

Jesus has shown us the way of obedient self-oblation.
Now we are invited to follow in the way, and go all the way
with him who is the Way—the Way of life *through* death. "A
servant is not greater than his master. If they have persecuted me, they will persecute you" (John 15:20).

So Luke, in the second volume of his record, deliberately
parallels the self-offering of Paul, who willingly goes up to
Jerusalem to suffering and the risk of death, with Jesus who
had taken the same path.

The central clause in Paul's speech, as recorded by Dr.
Luke, is highly significant. "I do not account my life of any
value nor as precious to myself." Here is the true apostle
and the shepherd who is willing to lay down his life for the
sheep. The new way of life for others, which was initiated
on the cross of Calvary, has already caught on. The priestly
way of life for others has entered the world through Calvary; now we see Paul's offering and obedient discipleship
and the same offering by St. Ignatius. It will not be long before what happened *somewhere*, once upon a time, will begin
to happen *everywhere* all the time, until the end of time. This
is the new economy and order which is overturning the old
order of "every man for himself." Calvary, Miletus, Antioch—
they are all signposts on the royal highway back to heaven.
They stand at the real crossroads in the long, evolutionary
journey of the human race from the kingdoms of this world
to the kingdom of our Christ and of his God.

The Witness of the Saints

SAINT IGNATIUS OF ANTIOCH (ca. 35–ca. 107)

In so many ways, Ignatius patterned his life on that of
St. Paul. He wrote letters to the churches at the centers of

Christian life in his day. In one of these, to the Romans, he suggests that he had formerly been a pagan and a persecutor of the Christian church. Little, however, is known of his early life, except that as bishop of Antioch, under the persecution of the emperor Trajan, he left Antioch under arrest, bound for death in Rome. The bishop and the soldiers boarded a ship at Seleucia (a seaport near Antioch) and took a slow route along the southern and western shores of Asia Minor and only then in a direct voyage to Rome, where the bishop was to meet his death in the Colosseum.

The first stop on that journey was at Smyrna, where Ignatius met his former fellow disciple, the saintly Polycarp. From there he went on to Ephesus to meet Bishop Onesimus (just possibly the Onesimus of Paul's letter to Philemon). As Ignatius journeyed, he wrote his famous letters, seven in all, to the churches, including his last letter to the Christians in Rome.

As the saint approached Rome, the Christians from the various congregations and churches would come out to meet him. He would kneel down and pray with them, but always pleading with them not to hinder his ultimate martyrdom in Rome.

According to legend, he arrived in Rome on December 20, the last day of the public games. He was hurried off immediately to the amphitheater and martyred before the fierce and hysterical crowd.

His letters bear the authority of words from a martyr— words written in blood. Clearly, he was passionately dedicated to Christ and was consumed with a deep desire to die for Christ in imitation of the Christ who had first died for him. He held a forceful and powerful doctrine of the humanity and the divinity of Christ—"our God, Jesus Christ," as he constantly refers to Christ. The life of Christ is for Ignatius most evident in the eucharistic bread—"the bread that is the flesh of Jesus Christ, this flesh which has suffered for our sins." And even in those early days of Christianity, he sees the office of bishop "as the Lord" in the church and the focus of unity in an expanding and diversifying church.

Our Experience

Christians should live their lives in such a way that death

completes and consummates the offering and the oblation of a lifetime of daily surrender to God. Put another way, the whole of life is a daily rehearsal for the ultimate and great "Amen"—that ultimate "yes" to God. "I can only unite myself to the will of God (as endured passively)," wrote Teilhard de Chardin, "when all my strength is spent." The faithful during the Middle Ages used to pray that the Christian would die while receiving communion. Surely there is an even higher aspiration: to seek the grace to make our death such an offering of obedience, that it is itself the ultimate communion—the consummation of all our life and in one sense our first, *real* communion with God.

That does not mean that we should refuse medical help and will ourselves to death. (Equally, it does not mean that we should "strive" to keep alive: it is a fine point of balance). The gospels show two complementary attitudes of Jesus towards his death. In the garden of Gethsemane, we see him shrinking from the prospect of death and exploring every other possibility. That is healthy. Then, especially in John's Gospel, there is a distinct turning point when we see Christ going out to meet his cross, carrying it himself and mounting it, in fulfillment of his offering and his obedience to the will of the Father.

"Father, into thy hands I commend my spirit," spells out the ultimate "amen," the final *fiat mihi*. Yet, that was only possible in his death, because his whole life had been a daily rehearsal for Gethsemane and Calvary. For the prayer "Father, into thy hands I commend my spirit" is not only a prayer for the end of the day, but also a prayer for the beginning and at every hour of every day of our life. We shall need to learn how to say yes (amen) to God in small everyday ways as well as in big ways and on big days; in our youth as well as in our old age; in success as well as in failure; in health as well as in sickness. At every point on the journey, that great, little word must be on our lips, because it was first inscribed as *fiat mihi* on our hearts. The vocabulary is incidental, depending perhaps upon your language preference. It might be "amen" or "yes"; "right on," *fiat mihi*, or just plain, old-fashioned "O.K." In the second letter to the Corinthians, Paul says, "For the Son of God, Jesus Christ...was not Yes or No:

but in him it is always Yes. For all the promises of God find their Yes in him. That is why we utter the Amen through him, to the glory of God" (2 Cor. 1:19–20). We will only be able to say that ultimate "yes," if our life is hidden with God in Christ and is an echo of his once, for all, great "Amen" to God on Calvary.

The pilgrimage of Ignatius from Antioch to his death in Rome was a gloriously crescendoing "Amen" to God in an age when it was almost more important as Christian witness for men and women to die for Christ than it was for them to live for Christ. Today, in most parts of the world, it is rather different: "for Christian witness demands that we undergo life as much as we undergo death, if not more" (Teilhard de Chardin).

Yet, whether we live or whether we die, today, tomorrow, or in many years, the bottom line of the Christian faith is learning to say, as well as to live, (with increasing abandonment to the Divine Providence)—Amen, Yes, O.K., so that in the end, whenever, wherever, or however death comes, it will be truly and finally O.K. Amen.

THE EIGHTH DAY

After this I looked, and behold, a great multitude which no man could number, from every nation, from all tribes and peoples and tongues, standing before the throne and before the Lamb, clothed in white robes, with palm branches in their hands, and crying out with a loud voice, "Salvation belongs to our God who sits upon the throne, and to the Lamb!" And all the angels stood round the throne and round the elders and the four living creatures, and they fell on their faces before the throne and worshipped God, saying, "Amen! Blessing and glory and wisdom and thanksgiving and honor and power and might be to our God for ever and ever! Amen!"

Then one of the elders addressed me, saying, "Who are these, clothed in white robes, and whence have they come?" I said to him, "Sir, you know." And he said to me, "These are they who have come out of the great tribulation; they have washed their robes and made them white in the blood of the Lamb. Therefore are they before the throne of God, and serve him day and night within his temple; and he who sits upon the throne will shelter them with his presence. They shall hunger no more, neither thirst any more; the sun shall not strike them, nor any scorching heat. For the Lamb in the midst of the throne will be their shepherd, he will guide them to springs of living water; and God will wipe away every tear from their eyes." (Rev. 7:9–17)

The Witness of Scripture

John paints for us an unforgettable picture of a huge crowd of people, from every nation on earth, who are now caught up in the bliss, the glory, and the worship of heaven.

The diversity is the first thing which strikes us as we share in John's vision. We see a truly catholic community from all nations and kindred and peoples and tongues. Their unity is in the dynamic of their worship and their singlemindedness—the worship due to one God who is in all and above all. We see this body of people corporately, which is not the same thing as seeing them collectively.

The redeemed are dressed in white robes, we are told. The Greek word signifies long robes, the very opposite, in fact, of workaday overalls. This is full party dress!

The palms in their hands are emblems of victory and triumph. But, clearly, they are not celebrating *their* victory, but his. Salvation is not the property of the saints: it is God's gift and belongs to him and to those to whom he chooses to give it.

Their principal occupation, from start to finish, is worship—a worship freely offered from a free heart. "Oh, for a heart to praise my God, a heart from sin set free!"

And who are they all? These are they who literally have been *through* it! But now all of their desires are satisfied in the One who is their hearts' desire. They will know no hunger. They will not thirst. Typical physical ills which afflict humanity on earth are taken as symbols. In a word, whatever the torment, the divine community is now free from it. God's tender concern makes complete provision for all our needs.

How can this be? It is because the shepherd is also the lamb. The word in Greek used for "guide" is the word applied to a shepherd. Here we see a reversal of roles. John is making the point that Christ, in the sacrifice of himself, has made provision for all the needs in the way that a shepherd would normally do. Jesus is both the good shepherd and the sacrificial lamb. He is all, in all.

The Witness of the Saints

The observance of a day to celebrate All Saints—known, and unknown, named or anonymous—was originally fixed on May 13, the day for the dedication of the Pantheon in Rome. Certainly, such a feast day was observed as early as the fourth century. In the eighth century, we have evidence of a special feast day on April 20 as the day for celebrating "all the saints of the whole of Europe."

However, we are on firm ground by the year 800, for we know that by that date, Alcuin was in the habit of observing All Saints Day on November 1.

So it is that the church has recognized the place of saints and holiness within the total life and witness of God's holy people, and has rightly set aside a day each year to celebrate the saints and to thank God for the gift of the saints in every generation.

Our Experience

The saints are the best proof there is that the resurrection is true, that grace triumphs over sin, and that love casts out fear.

If the principal end of humanity is worship, then it will be in the true worship of the true God that we shall find our freedom and our fulfillment. To sin means to miss the point of it all. Therefore, in a sense, a sinful life has not discovered the point of it all which is true worship offered to the one God.

If we were made for the worship of God, as the Bible and the church teach, then it means that come hell or high water we shall find someone, somewhere to worship, somehow! The danger is that we shall worship false gods, or worship the creature rather than the Creator, as St. Paul warns us in his epistle to the Romans. When we do this, we are drawn into compulsive behavior, as the object of our worship cannot ultimately satisfy the needs we have for worship. It is then that we fall into bondage and lose our freedom.

The significant difference between the worship of the one true God and the worship of all those false gods is simply that, as we worship the true God, he gives us back our freedom which we lost in the false worship of the Garden of Eden. In God's worship and service, the saints have found true freedom. They have found their strength and their joy in him who is the ultimate object of their love as well as the cause of all their joy.

"Free at last, free at last; thank God Almighty, I'm free at last."

> Exceedingly odd is the means by which God
> Has provided our path to the heavenly shore—
> Of the girls from whose line the true light was to shine
> There was one an adulteress, one was a whore:
> There was Tamar who bore—what we all should deplore—
> A fine pair of twins to her father-in-law,
> And Rahab the harlot, her sins were as scarlet,
> As red as the thread that she hung from the door;
> Yet alone of her nation she came to salvation
> And lived to be mother of Boaz of yore—
> And he married Ruth, a Gentile uncouth,
> In a manner quite counter to biblical lore:
> And of her there did spring blessed David the King,
> Who walked on his palace one evening and saw
> The wife of Uriah, from whom he did sire
> A baby that died—oh and princes a score:
> And a mother unmarried it was too that carried
> God's Son, and him laid in a manger of straw,
> That the moral might wait at the heavenly gate
> While the sinners and publicans go in before,
> Who have not earned their place, but received it by grace,
> And have found there a righteousness not of the law.
>   (Michael Goulder)

So the last word should, perhaps, be with one of the saints who is most conspicuous in the history of the saints, and who indicates perhaps most clearly the power of grace and of true worship. Set free from bondage to creation, for free worship and love of the Creator, Augustine looks to the worship of heaven where we shall know the true freedom and joy of holiness.

"The important thing is that the seventh day will be our Sabbath, whose end will not be an evening, but rather the Lord's Day, an eighth day as it were, which is to last forever, a day consecrated by the resurrection of Christ, foreshadowing the eternal rest not only of the Spirit but of the body also. There we shall be still and we shall see; we shall see and we shall love; we shall love and we shall praise. Behold what will be, in the end, without end! For what is our end, but to reach that kingdom which has no end?"

(Augustine)

Amen! Even so, come Lord Jesus!

44 000
5.99